RECONNECTING WITH GOD

12 STEPS TO REVITALISE YOUR WALK WITH GOD

KEVIN SIMINGTON

Smart Faith Press

RECONNECTING WITH GOD
12 Steps To A Revitalised Walk With God

Includes a Study Guide for small groups and sermon outlines for preachers

© Copyright 2021 Kevin Simington

All rights reserved. No part of this publication may be reproduced, stored in a retrieval system or transmitted in any form by any means electronic, mechanical, photocopying, recording or otherwise, without the prior written permission of the author.

Unless otherwise specified, Scripture quotations are from the New International Version Bible, copyright © 1973, 1978, 1984, 2011, Zondervan, Grand Rapids, Michigan, USA.

EDITORS: Sandra Simington, John Crooks

PUBLISHER: Smart Faith Press

SMART FAITH PRESS

✽ Created with Vellum

CONTENTS

Preface   v

PART I
CONNECTING TO JESUS

1. Diagnose Your Disconnection   3
2. Understand The Wonder Of The Cross   25
3. Trust In Jesus As Saviour   41
4. Submit To Jesus As Lord   59
5. Serve Jesus The King   81

PART II
CONNECTING IN PRAYER

6. Confront The Struggle Of Prayer   101
7. Dare To Pray In Faith   115
8. Pray With Persistence   131

PART III
CONNECTING WITH GOD'S WORD

9. Trust The Bible's Reliability   145
10. Trust The Bible's Inspiration   163
11. Be Committed To Reading God's Word   175

PART IV
CONNECTING WITH GOD'S FAMILY

12. Love Me, Love My Family   193
13. No Magic Pill   209

FREE SERMON OUTLINES	215
Also by Kevin Simington	217
7 Reasons To Believe	219
Finding God When He Seems To Be Hiding	221
Making Sense of the Bible	223
No More Monkey Business:	225
The Little Book of Church Leadership	227
Welcome To The Universe	229
Someone Else's Life	231
The Starpath Series	233
Connect With Kevin Simington	235
About the Author	237
Notes	239

PREFACE

We live in an age of superficial connection. We share photos of our morning coffee on Facebook and Instagram, but we don't share the deepest parts of our hearts and lives. We have lots of Facebook 'friends' and Instagram followers, but very few significant friends who truly know us, whom we trust to walk beside us through life's deepest valleys. Many people today regularly use social media to hook up with total strangers for casual sex and seem to regard it little differently than ordering fast food. Technology has made our social connection with others easier and faster today, but much more superficial.

This plague of superficiality has also impacted our connection with God. A variety of research indicates that the average Christian spends much less time reading the Bible and praying than Christians did fifty years ago. Attendance at church gatherings has also become more sporadic and uncommitted. The average Christian's relationship with God has become marginalised, pushed to the side, less important, less central to their everyday lives than it used to be. They are connected to social media, but relatively disconnected from God.

This book is about reconnecting with God: connecting deeply and profoundly. It is about moving beyond the superficial connection that you might have drifted into and developing a relationship with God that is truly transformative. The principles taught in this book are also relevant for people who have not yet entered into a relationship with God and who are ready to set out on that journey.

This is a very practical book. At the end of each chapter there are prompts for personal reflection as well as Bible readings and discussion questions for groups. *Reconnecting with God* has been specifically written with group study in mind and would be an ideal resource for your home group, cell group, life group or Bible study group to use.

For preachers who want to link their Sunday sermons with their church's small group studies, there is a link at the back of the book to download FREE sermon outlines for each of the 12 topics.

May this book enable you to tap into the most powerful wireless connection in the world; a life-transforming connection with your Creator.

PART I

CONNECTING TO JESUS

1

DIAGNOSE YOUR DISCONNECTION

This book is designed to help you reconnect with God. Perhaps you have never really had a connection with God up until this point in your life, but you are now interested in finding out what this Christianity business is all about. Welcome! You've come to the right place! The practical steps in this book will help you discover a relationship with your Creator that will transform your life, now and forever.

On the other hand, you may be a Christian who has been in the faith for many years, but your relationship with God has grown a little stale. The 'zing' has gone. You're in the right place, too! The guidelines presented in this book will help you to revitalise your walk with the Lord.

Whatever your situation, I want to begin our journey at the same point. The first step in either connecting with God for the first time or re-energising that connection, is to go back to the beginning and ensure that we understand the foundational basis of any connection with God and the primary disruptor of that connection.

It is at this point that the Christian faith is most commonly misunderstood.

The vast majority of people believe that being a Christian is all about living a good enough life so that you are acceptable to God. If I was to conduct a survey in a shopping centre or on a street corner and ask passers-by, *"Assuming there is a Heaven, what must you do to go to Heaven?"*, almost everyone would talk about living a good life or obeying the Ten Commandments or something similar. Even regular church-goers can have this view. The problem is, it simply isn't true.

Anyone wanting to connect with God must get rid of any concept of relating to God on the basis of merit. Romans 3:20 says:

> "No one will be justified in God's sight by works of the law. For the law merely brings awareness of sin."

This is an essential starting point that everyone must reach if they are to have any chance of having a relationship with God at all. It is also an essential truth that you must come back to if you are to re-establish a connection with God that may have waned or grown stale. It is absolutely crucial that we start with this fundamental assertion: that no one will ever reach a point where they are good enough to be acceptable to God.

Yet this concept of one's own meritorious goodness and, therefore, one's worthiness of a place in God's kingdom, is endemic throughout society. The average person is quietly confident in their relative goodness and their acceptability to God. Donald Trump typified the average person's attitude regarding their own self-assessed merit when he made the following comment in a CNN TV interview entitled *"Trump: One on One"*:

"Why do I have to repent? Why do I have to ask for forgiveness? I don't make any mistakes. I work hard and I'm an honest person. I try to lead a life where I don't have to ask God for forgiveness."

This is the typical attitude of most people. The vast majority of people consider that they have not done anything too horrendously bad and, therefore, they must be acceptable to God just as they are. This is an extremely dangerous view to hold because it results in false confidence that is totally out of alignment with God's declaration about our *true* condition, as revealed in his Word.

FALSE VIEW OF SELF-RIGHTEOUSNESS

The view that *"I am acceptable to God, just as I am"* is based upon four misleading premises, all of which involve the concept of meritorious salvation (salvation on the basis of one's own merit):

- Delusional Perfection
- Comparative Righteousness
- Pass Mark Salvation
- Transactional Atonement

These premises are worth examining in detail, as most people hold one or more of these views.

1. DELUSIONAL PERFECTION

I sometimes encounter people who claim they have never sinned. In fact, this is a surprisingly common view. I remember a conversation I once had with a young woman one Sunday morning, immediately after a sermon that I had preached on the topic of sin and our need for God's forgiveness. The conversation went roughly as follows:

Carmen (not her real name): *"I don't need God's grace. I've never sinned."*

Me: *"Really? Never?"*

Carmen: *"Yep. Never!"*

Me: *"What about the 10 commandments?"*

Carmen: *"I've kept all of them."*

Me: *"Really? What about the first two? They talk about placing God before anything or anyone else in your life. Can you honestly say you've always done that?"*

Carmen: *"Well, not those two, but I've kept all the others."*

Me: *"OK. What about the next one: don't misuse the name of God. Have you ever used God's name as a swear word?"*

Carmen: *"Yes, I suppose so."*

I continued with the rest of the commandments that talk about our need to honour our parents, to not murder (redefined by Jesus as hating others), to not commit adultery (redefined by Jesus as looking lustfully at others), to not steal, to not lie and to not covet the possessions of others. At the end of our discussion Carmen admitted that she scored zero out of ten!

Those who claim that they have never sinned usually hold that view because they have never really bothered to examine how God defines 'sin' in His Word. They tend to define sin very narrowly, as only relating to serious misdemeanours such as murder. But the Bible tells us that we sin when we break ANY of God's commandments – not just the ones we regard as 'serious'. The Old Testament contains 613 commandments of God; a moral code which precisely defines how he wants us to live. While some of these commandments no longer apply to us today (such as the ceremonial laws that were specifically for the

Jews), the majority of moral laws are still relevant, as they are repeated in the New Testament. Furthermore, in the New Testament, Jesus added to these commandments, often raising them to a whole new level.

> "You have heard that it was said, 'Do not commit adultery.' But I tell you that anyone who looks at a woman lustfully has already committed adultery with her in his heart." (Matthew 5:27)

> "You have heard it said, 'Do not murder' and 'Anyone who murders will be subject to judgment.' But I tell you that anyone who is angry with his brother will be subject to judgment." (Matthew 5:21)

When we properly understand the commandments of God, it becomes impossible for a person to maintain a belief in their own sinless perfection. Put simply, the person who claims never to have sinned is delusional.

2. COMPARATIVE RIGHTEOUSNESS

Going back to my conversation with Carmen, once she eventually conceded that she had broken all of the Ten Commandments, she still refused to accept that she was a sinner in need of forgiveness. She said something like:

"But haven't done anything really bad. I mean, I'm a much better person than most people!"

In one sense she was probably right. She may well be a much better person than most people. But that is not the measuring stick by which we are meant to gauge our own righteousness. Comparing ourselves to others doesn't give us a reliable reading on our relative goodness. If I compare myself to a serial murderer in a maximum-security prison, I am a pretty good person by comparison. But if I compare myself to Mother Teresa (1910 – 1997) who lived a large part of her life in the slums of India, caring for the homeless, feeding orphans, and working with sufferers of leprosy, HIV/AIDS and tuberculosis, I am a selfish, lazy, greedy, materialistic capitalist by comparison! My perceived self-righteousness varies enormously, depending on who I am comparing myself to. And even if it happens to be true that I am morally more upright than the average person, is this really a reliable measurement? All it means is that I am *relatively* more righteous than most people. But is there a way of determining my righteousness *objectively*? To whom or what am I to compare myself in order to get a true *objective* gauge of the state of my character? Jesus tells us, very clearly and simply:

> "Be perfect as your Heavenly Father is perfect" (Matthew 5:48)

We are meant to compare ourselves to God, not to other people. The measuring stick for gauging our own goodness is not the shifting sands of imperfect humanity, but the rock-solid, unchanging character of our Holy God. And if you want to know what God's character looks like in practice, look at the life of Jesus, who lived among us as God in the flesh. He lived a completely sinless life; perfect in love, kindness, compassion, moral integrity and holiness. Compared to him, we all fall way short!

Carmen's problem was that she was comparing herself to others, instead of comparing herself to the Holy God and his perfect standards. And her attitude is typical of the misguided concept that most people have when evaluating their own self-righteousness. The average person is comparing themselves to 'bad people' – people guilty of horrible crimes. Compared to those people, most of us look pretty good, don't we? We haven't murdered anyone or committed any serious offences. We might have copped the occasional speeding ticket or parking fine, but we haven't done anything too seriously wrong. We've loved our families, been diligent workers, lived as responsible citizens and not cheated (too much!) on our tax returns. We are basically good people. Most people therefore assume, *"Surely God can't have a problem with me?"*

Yes, he can. And yes, he does. A very big problem, in fact.

You see, God isn't comparing you to other people and their obviously lower standards. God compares you to himself and evaluates you against his own perfect standards, compared to which we all fall hopelessly short.

3. PASS MARK SALVATION

An associated belief regarding the question of our acceptability to God is what I call 'pass mark salvation'. After many years as a church minister, I became a Christian Educator, teaching Biblical Studies and Studies of Religion in a Christian high school. When I set my students an essay or an exam, I would often be asked, *"Sir, what's the pass mark?"* I tended to resist setting a formal pass mark, so, by default, most students assumed that it was 51%. If you have studied at University, you would know that most subjects require you to attain a minimum standard or aggregate mark in order to pass the course and progress to the next subject. We are used to the system of 'pass marks' in education and also in many vocations.

Many people assume that God must use a similar system to determine entry into Heaven. They believe that as long as they have obeyed God's commandments more often than they have broken them, they have 'passed'. They have been good more often than they have been bad. This assumes a pass mark of at least 51%.

Out of curiosity one day (many years ago), I conducted a random survey of people in my local community, asking them:

"In terms of our level of goodness, what do you think God's pass-mark is for entry into Heaven?"

I got varying responses, ranging from 50% to 75%. Once a person gave me their answer, I would then respectfully challenge their response:

"So, you think you can be really bad 50% of the time and still get into heaven?" (or 40% of the time or 30% ...etc.)

Then I would ask them how they arrived at that figure. Usually, they would admit that it was just a guess. I would then say something like:

"Wouldn't it be good to know for sure what the pass mark is, instead of just guessing?"

Once they agreed, I would continue:

"Well, I've got some good news and some bad news. The good news is that God hasn't left us in the dark about this. He has actually told us what the pass mark is. The bad news is that it's much higher than you guessed."

I would then read the words of Jesus, from Matthew's Gospel:

> *"Be **perfect** as your Heavenly Father is perfect."* (Matthew 5:48)

Ouch! That is shockingly high. In fact, it's impossible, isn't it? Surely no one can achieve that level of perfection! As a matter of fact, that is precisely the point Jesus is making. He is demolishing our false confidence in our own self-righteousness. He is explaining that however good you may think you are, you are still a long way short of the standard that God demands. The message of the gospel starts with very bad news: the news that no one will ever be acceptable to God based upon their own merit, because we all fall short of God's perfect standard.

It is at this point that we really need to talk about that three-letter word, 'sin'. (Yes, that old chestnut). 'Sin' is not a popular word these days. In fact, the concept has gone out of vogue in many churches. Preachers tend to avoid using the word, for fear of turning people off. The word 'sin' carries all sorts of negative connotations of old fashioned 'fire and brimstone' sermons and narrow-minded fundamentalist judgmentalism. But Jesus and the New Testament writers had no such qualms about using the word in the first century. The word 'sin' appears 431 times in the Bible, including 104 times in the New Testament. Why does the Bible speak about sin so much? Because it is the thing that separates mankind from God and, unless the problem is dealt with, it will separate each of us from God eternally.

The New Testament word for 'sin' is the word, "hamartia" (ἁμαρτία), and it literally means "to fall short of a target." In fact, it was the word used to describe the shortfall of an archer's arrow which not only failed to hit the bullseye but didn't even make it as far as the target. When Jesus and the New Testament writers spoke about the problem of our sin, this is exactly the concept they are referring to. God's 'pass-mark' into Heaven, the 'target' we are meant to aim for, is absolute perfection. But all of us fall hopelessly short of that standard. Not only do we not hit the bullseye, we don't even make it as far as the target! This is what is meant in Romans 3:23:

> "For all have sinned and <u>fall short</u> of the glory [perfection] of God"
> (Romans 3:23)

At this point, some people will raise an objection: surely God is being unreasonable in insisting on perfection. No one is perfect! How can God insist on such an unrealistic standard?

In one sense, the answer is quite simple: if God lowers his standard and allows sin to enter Heaven, it will surely ruin the place! Heaven would no longer be perfect; in fact, it would be more of the same – just like life on Earth, except it would last forever. I don't know about you, but that doesn't appeal to me very much!

But there is a deeper reason for God's insistence on perfect obedience to his commands. Sin, at its core, is rebellion against God's rule over our lives. When we break his commands, we are effectively saying, *"I don't recognise your right to tell me what to do. I'll do what I want, not want you want."* The Bible declares that it is this attitude of rebellion that lies at the heart of our problem:

> *"We all, like sheep, have gone astray, each of us has <u>turned to our own way</u>." (Isaiah 53:6. Also quoted in 1 Peter 2:25)*

This verse gets to the very core of the matter. Sin is not merely an accumulation of individual misdemeanours; it is essentially an attitude of rebellion against God. We have turned our backs on God and *"turned to our own way."* When we sin, we are effectively rejecting God's Kingship and making ourselves King. And people who have rejected God's Kingship have forfeited their right to be part of his kingdom.

Someone might say, *"But I obey God's commands 70% of the time! I obey him as King 70% of the time! Surely that's good enough!"*

No, it isn't. Can you imagine saying to a prospective employer, *"I will turn up for work and submit to you as my employer 70% of workdays, but the other 30% of workdays I will do my own thing and won't show up"*? Or can you imagine saying to a prospective football coach, *"I will show up for practice and for games 70% of the time, but the other 30%, I'll take off and have some 'me time'"*? The employer or football coach would simply say to you, *"In that case don't bother turning up at all!"*

God wants to populate his kingdom with people who will consistently honour him as King, and that is why he insists on perfect obedience as the standard. Compared to this, the average person's concept of "pass mark salvation" falls woefully short.

The problem for all of us, of course, is that we are completely incapable of ever reaching God's standard of perfection:

> "For all have sinned and fall short of the glory [perfection] of God" (Romans 3:23)

We will examine this problem later, but firstly, we need to discuss an additional false view of meritorious salvation.

4. TRANSACTIONAL ATONEMENT

Transactional atonement refers to the view that we can somehow make up for our many acts of disobedience by doing lots of good deeds. According to this view, our many good deeds will impress God and cause him to overlook whatever bad things we have done. Furthermore, as long as we have done more good deeds than bad, as long as our ledger is in the black – in positive balance – we are in spiritual 'profit' and are, therefore, acceptable to God. In a sense, this view says that we can 'buy' our way out of trouble through good works.

Once again, this is a very common view. Unfortunately, it is completely wrong, for several reasons.

Firstly, at a very practical level, it simply doesn't make judicial sense. Can you imagine if our courts operated like this? Suppose a serial murderer was on trial for the murder of three people. His defence counsel doesn't contest this, but instead, presents a long list of the defendant's many good deeds; hundreds of hours spent volunteering for charity, teaching

Sunday school and working for free in the local school canteen. Can you imagine the public outrage if the judge then said, "Since you have done more good things than bad, I will let you off. I pronounce you not guilty. You are free to go." Such a judge would be removed from the bench very quickly! Why? Because no amount of good deeds can atone for the crimes that were committed. Good deeds aren't a magic eraser that 'undo' the crimes or expunge the record of a person's wrong-doing. Our judicial system doesn't work that way. Crimes cannot be overlooked simply because a person has also done some good things. Crime must be dealt with and justice must be done.

The same is true in regard to God. He is a just God, and sin must be dealt with. Our supposed good deeds aren't some kind of spiritual eraser that expunges the record of sin from our souls. We can't buy our way out of trouble with God by waiving the currency of our good deeds in the air. This is why the Bible says:

> "No one will be justified in God's sight by works of the law." (Romans 3:20)

Secondly, this false transactional view of atonement also fails to appreciate the vast record of our wrongdoing. The previous example of the Ten Commandments is a good starting point for our understanding. Despite the fact that I don't know you, the reader, at all, I can say with absolutely confidence that you have broken every single one of the Ten Commandments. Furthermore, you haven't merely broken them once or twice. You have probably broken them thousands of times. The Ten Commandments tell us to put God before everything and everyone else in our lives. They tell us to turn away from lying, cheating, dishonesty, jealousy, coveting, slander, lust and hatred, and to always honour our parents. There probably isn't a single day in your life when you haven't broken at least one of those commandments!

Furthermore, the New Testament raises God's standards to an even higher level. We are told that even failing help to someone who is in need is a sin (Matthew 25:31-46). That's right! Simply keeping my head down and ignoring the needs of others around me – even though I'm not doing anything obviously 'bad' – is a sin in God's eyes.

With that understanding, our sins accumulate on a daily basis. A selfish action. A lustful thought. A proud attitude. A cutting remark. An act of unforgiveness. A smutty joke. A distortion of the truth. An act of deception. A judgmental attitude. A harsh word of gossip. A derisory put-down. A snide comment. Lying to cover up for our mistakes. Fudging the truth. Exaggerating. Cheating our employer by not working hard enough or taking longer breaks than we are entitled to. Failing to love and respect someone as they deserve. Failing to help someone in need. The list is almost endless.

Most of us would easily clock up at least three sins each day. Over the course of an average lifetime, that amounts to at least 70,000 sins! This is why anyone claiming to have *"lived a good life"* is only fooling themselves.

Imagine a criminal who has committed 70,000 crimes, standing in the dock of a courtroom. Picture the scene. The evidence is presented to the judge, and it is unequivocal. The man really has committed 70,000 crimes! The judge then asks him, *"Before I pass sentence, do you have anything to say for yourself?"* Incredibly, the criminal sticks out his chest, looks the judge in the eye and says, *"Your honour, I've lived a good life. Look at all these other good things I've done."* It would be an utterly ridiculous claim for him to make, wouldn't it? He would be laughed out of court! Yet this is the foolish claim that many people make in regard to their own self-perceived righteousness. Despite having committed tens of thousands of sins over their lifetime, repeatedly and blatantly breaking God's commandments and living self-centred lives, they naïvely insist that they have lived a good life. They believe that the good things they have done can buy their way out of the unimaginably huge debt of sin they have accumulated.

This is why transactional atonement simply doesn't work. Those who are trusting in their own good deeds to get them out of trouble with God have misunderstood the nature of God's justice and have vastly underestimated the record of their own wrongdoing.

THE REAL PICTURE

In the first few chapters of the biblical book of Romans, the Apostle Paul is addressing the very same false views of self-righteousness that I have just outlined. He is writing to the church in Rome where these kinds of views have taken root: the concepts of delusional perfection, comparative righteousness, pass mark salvation and transactional atonement.

Listen again to what Paul says to the people who have started to trust in their own righteousness for their salvation:

> "There is no one righteous, not even one. [11] There is no one who understands, no one who seeks God. [12] All have turned away, they have together become worthless; there is no one who does good, not even one. [13] Their throats are open graves; their tongues practice deceit. The venom of vipers is on their lips. [14] Their mouths are full of cursing and bitterness. [15] Their feet are swift to shed blood; [16] ruin and misery lie in their wake, [17] and the way of peace they have not known. [18] There is no fear of God before their eyes. [19] Now we know that whatever the law says, it says to those who are under the law, so that every mouth may be silenced and the whole world

held accountable to God. [20] Therefore no one will be justified in his sight by works of the law. For the law merely brings awareness of sin." (Romans 3:10-20)

These are strong words, aren't they? They are not happy, comforting words. I suspect that Paul was not winning over many new friends in this passage. So, why was he so negative? Why so critical? Because he wants to make it crystal clear that we can't save ourselves! He wants us to be absolutely convinced that we are backing a losing horse if we are trusting in our own good works to save us. Notice his opening remark:

> "There is no one righteous, not even one ... there is no one who does good, not even one." (verses 11-12)

That's right. No one. Not you. Not me. Not the Pope nor Billy Graham. How can this be? He explains:

> "All have turned away ..." (Verse 12)

In other words, we are, at heart, rebels. Our natural tendency is to disobey God and go our own way. The prophet Isaiah described this condition accurately:

> "We all, like sheep, have gone astray, each of us has turned to our own way" (Isaiah 53:6; also quoted in 1 Peter 2:25)

You see, my problem and your problem is not merely that we have committed a large number of sins. Our problem goes much deeper than that. The individual sins we commit are merely the outward symptoms of a deeper malaise. The Bible teaches that we are all born with a sinful nature, an inbuilt bias that leads us consistently and inexorably toward disobedience and rebellion against God's perfect moral code. Every human being is born with this bias; a hereditary tendency to disobey God that has been passed down from generation to generation:

> "Surely I was sinful at birth, sinful from the time my mother conceived me." (Psalm 51:5)

The Bible says that our sinful nature enslaves us, so that we are incapable of going against our tendency toward disobedience of God's commands:

> "I am unspiritual, sold as a slave to sin ... For what I want to do I do not do, but what I hate I do ... For I know that good itself does not dwell in me, that is, in my sinful nature. For I have the desire to do what is good, but I cannot carry it out. For I do not do the good I want to do, but the evil I do not want to do—this I keep on doing." (Romans 7:15-19)

The extent and depth of our sin is no trivial thing. The Bible's testimony is clear. We are not basically good people who make occasional moral blunders: we are consumed and controlled by our sinful natures. We are sinful at the very core of our being, and out of that core flows a daily stream of individual sin: lust, greed, selfishness, pride, envy, hatred, judgmentalism, unforgiveness, jealousy, slander, lies, gossip, cheating, stealing. And that's just Monday mornings! Then on Monday afternoons ...

If you are in any doubt as to your own complete sinfulness and your desperate standing before your Creator, a quick read of these Bible verses will set you straight:

> "The Lord saw how great man's wickedness on the earth had become, and that every inclination of the thoughts of their heart was only evil all the time." (Genesis 6:5)

> "There is no one on earth who is righteous, no one who does what is right and never sins." (Ecclesiastes 7:20)

> "There is no one who understands, no one who seeks God. All have turned away; they have together become worthless; there is no one who does good, not even one. Their throats are open graves; their tongues practice deceit. The venom of vipers is on their lips. Their mouths are full of cursing and bitterness. Their feet are swift to shed blood; ruin and misery mark their ways, and the way of peace they do not know. There is no fear of God before their eyes." (Romans 3:11-18)

> "All have sinned and fall short of the glory of God." (Romans 3:23)

> "We all, like sheep, have gone astray, each of us has turned to our own way." (Isaiah 53:6 and 1 Peter 2:25)

Indeed, as I have already explained, this last verse gets to the very heart of the matter. Sin is not merely an accumulation of individual misdemeanours; it is essentially an attitude of rebellion against God. We have turned our backs on God and *"turned to our own way."*

The Bible is unequivocal: our souls are not predominantly white with a few specks of sin that our benign Creator will somehow overlook. No. They are stained black with the huge and dreadful record of our daily wrongdoing, brought forth from this attitude of rebellion. We are not good people who make occasional moral blunders: we are bad people who do occasional good things, but even then, our good works are often tainted with pride and selfish motives (Isaiah 64:6). Such is the depth of our sinfulness.

Our complete inability to overcome this pervasive sinful nature means that we are utterly unable to save ourselves. There is nothing we can do to atone for the huge weight of our wrongdoing or somehow expunge its record from our souls. Any person who thinks they will be able to stand in God's presence on the Day of Judgment and claim to have *"lived a good life"* – to have perfectly obeyed all his commandments – is completely deluded.

> *"Every mouth will be silenced and the whole world held accountable to God. Therefore, no one will be declared righteous in God's sight by the works of the law; rather, through the law we become conscious of sin." (Romans 3:19-20)*

The ultimate consequence of our pervasive sinfulness, of this vast record of our wrongdoing, is separation from God, both now and forever:

> *"Your iniquities have separated you from your God; your sins have hidden his face from you so that he will not hear." (Isaiah 59:2)*

> *"For the wages of sin is death." (Romans 6:23)*

> *"... and they will go away to eternal punishment." (Matthew 25:46)*

The Bible paints a very grim picture of our predicament. Our sins have cut us off from God eternally and there is nothing we can do about it. The weight of our sin is so overwhelming, the record of our wrong-doing is so vast and extensive, that no amount of good deeds can take it away. We may regularly help little old ladies across the road, give to charity, volunteer for meals-on-wheels, or lead church services on a Sunday, but none of these things have the power to undo or expunge the vast and growing weight of sin that accumulates within our souls on a daily basis. We are unable to save ourselves. Our constant and pervasive sin has separated us from God.

This is the bad news of the gospel. And until you have fully understood that bad news, you will never truly appreciate the good news.

Let me add an important caveat to this topic. I am not saying that you aren't a nice person. The issue of 'niceness' doesn't come into it. Comparatively, (compared to the rest of humanity), you may well be a very nice person. As a general rule, you may treat others with kindness and respect. You might usually be compassionate, generous and forgiving. I know many people whom I would categorise as 'nice'. But even nice people have moments when they are unkind, disrespectful, unforgiving and lacking in compassion. They aren't nice all the time. And nice people sin in many other ways as well, perhaps in ways that are unseen, like pride or jealousy or lust. When we call someone 'nice' we are using the term comparatively. We mean they are nice in comparison to the average person. But, as we examined at the beginning of this chapter, our standard of comparison isn't other people, it is God himself, as portrayed in the perfect life of Jesus. The truth is that if we honestly compare ourselves to the perfect holiness of God, even the nicest of us is a sinner in desperate need of forgiveness. That is the bad news of the gospel.

The next chapter deals with the good news of the gospel; that God has stepped in to rescue us by punishing Jesus in our place, so that we can be freely forgiven and restored to fellowship with himself. But before we get to that good news, let me firstly ask you to reflect on the things we have examined so far.

PERSONAL REFLECTION

Read back over the four false views of self-righteousness, outlined in this chapter. Have you held any of these views up to this point in your life? Have you underestimated the extensive nature of your sin and its seriousness? Has your view of your own 'righteousness' been out of alignment with God's perception of you?

You might like to spend some time in prayer and reflection, confessing your sins and your utter dependence on God's grace.

GROUP DISCUSSION QUESTIONS

1. Share your thoughts and impressions from this chapter. What was new to you? What was helpful? What are you still unsure about?

Read Psalm 51:1-13

2. In verse 5, David declares that he was "sinful at birth". What do you think this means? (Some theologians make the distinction between "sinful" and "sinner". We are sinful at birth - born with a sinful nature - but we only become sinners when we first commit sin.)

3. The last part of verse 13 contains a subtle hint regarding the heart of our problem (from which all individual sins flow). What is it?

4. Get different group members to read the following verses: Genesis 6:5, Genesis 8:21, Romans 7:18. What are these verses all saying? Why does the Bible paint such a dim picture of human nature? Do you think it is possible for someone to be truly 'good' in God's eyes?

Read Isaiah 64:6

5. While it is true that many people do lots of very good things, such as volunteer for charities and give to the poor, what does this verse say about even these righteous acts? Why does it make such a grim proclamation? What is wrong with our acts of righteousness?

Read Isaiah 59:1-13

6. This passage is a graphic portrayal of the sinful nature that we are all afflicted with. Briefly highlight the examples of sin that this passage lists. The first part of verse 13 defines the very essence of our problem. What is it?

7. Verse 2 describes the ultimate result of sin. What is it? Do you have a problem with this consequence? Does it seem too harsh? Why is the consequence so severe?

Read Romans 7:14-25

8. In verses 14 to 24, Paul describes the predicament that we all find ourselves in. What is that predicament? (Verse 18 is a key verse).

9. Verse 25 pre-empts the good news of the Gospel (which we shall study next week). What does this verse tell us? How, precisely does Jesus solve our problem? Does this mean that Christians are no longer slaves to sin?

∽

2
UNDERSTAND THE WONDER OF THE CROSS

In the previous chapter I spelled out an important fundamental truth: we are all hopeless sinners – 'hopeless' in the sense of being completely unable to save ourselves.

But God has not left us in this state. He has provided a remedy. Through an act of unimaginably extravagant love, God has rescued us from our dire predicament. But the means of that rescue is quite shocking. It is deeply disturbing. It is not something we could make up if we were inventing a new religion. In fact, God's method of rescuing us seems so bizarre and barbaric, that it has become a stumbling block to many people.

Because, you see, God rescued us by killing his own Son – who, in fact, actually turns out to be an eternal part of himself.

I told you it was bizarre!

The death of the Son of God, Jesus Christ, on a cruel Roman cross 2,000 years ago was not an unfortunate end to an otherwise promising life. It was the primary purpose of Jesus' visit to our planet. He came to die a substitutionary death, allowing himself to be punished in our place, suffering the full wrath of

God's punishment for the sins of the whole world, so that God's justice could be satisfied and we could walk free. Mankind was on death row, pronounced guilty, sentenced to death and awaiting final execution, when the Son of God stepped in and died in our place. He took the punishment that we deserve, so that we could be forgiven. Somehow, by means of a spiritual transaction, the exact nature of which we can only dimly perceive, the death of Christ on the cross and his resurrection from the dead paid for the sins of the whole world.

> "He is the atoning sacrifice for our sins, and not only for ours but also for the sins of the whole world." (1 John 2:2)

As he hung on the cross, dying, God the Father punished God the Son, the innocent one, for every sin that ever has been committed and ever will be committed.

> "We all like sheep have gone astray, each of us has turned to our own way, but the Lord laid on him the iniquity of us all." (Isaiah 53:6)

> "He himself bore our sins in his body on the cross." (1 Peter 2:24)

THE MYSTERY OF THE CROSS

Why couldn't God just forgive us without the need for punishment? Why did he have to put Jesus to death in order to forgive us? After all, when we forgive someone, we don't insist on some kind of cruel retribution, do we? If someone does something very bad to me and then subsequently asks for forgiveness, I don't respond by saying, "I will forgive you, but in order to do that, I'm going to have to kill my dog." Or worse, "I'm going to have to whip my son." Or unimaginably worse, "I'm going to have to kill my son."

I'm not trying to be flippant or irreverent, but I want you to see how unusual this is. How extreme it is. How shocking it is.

So, let me ask the question again. *Why couldn't God just forgive us, without the need for any sacrifice?* The answer is that we may never fully understand the answer – at least not on this side of eternity. But there are some truths that will take us part way to an understanding of this mysterious spiritual transaction.

The Bible repeatedly states that there can be no forgiveness of sins without the shedding of blood (Leviticus 17:11 and Hebrews 9:22). In fact, the whole of the book of Hebrews, generally, and chapter nine in particular, expounds this mysterious truth. God is apparently not free to wave away our sins cheaply. There are serious consequences that must be faced and paid for. In a sense, this is exactly how our human judicial system works. Any judge who lets serious criminals walk free out of the goodness of his heart will soon find himself on the unemployment line. In fact, there is occasional outrage when a judge confers too lenient a sentence for a serious crime. As a society, we recognise that there needs to be appropriate consequences for those who break the law. We demand it. That is how justice works.

God apparently operates within a similar spiritual judicial system, although, in his case, it is not a system that has been imposed upon him from some outside source, but one which he, himself, has set in place. Sin must be paid for. Furthermore, this system of spiritual judicial consequences is not some arbitrary system of retribution that God has cooked up out of spite or unjustified anger. There is an inextricable link between sin and its inevitable consequence, death:

"For the wages of sin is death." (Romans 6:23)

This simple little statement is extremely important for our understanding of the necessity of the cross. This pronouncement of the ultimate consequence of sin – death (both physical and spiritual) – is not describing some kind of capricious over-reaction on God's part, such that we might complain, *"That seems a little too harsh, doesn't it?"*. No. We must understand this pronouncement in Romans 6:23 to be a declaration of the inextricable and inescapable consequence of sin. Sin actually kills the soul:

> *"The soul that sins shall die." (Ezekiel 18:20)*

In the same way that a fish that leaps out of water onto dry land will surely die, so too will the soul that turns its back on God. It is inevitable. Just as the fish is specifically designed to live in water, our souls are created to live within the life-giving dimension of a relationship with God, and as soon as we break that relationship through our sin, we begin to die:

> *"You were dead in your trespasses and sins" (Ephesians 2:1).*

Yes, but how does the sacrifice of Christ on the cross reverse or undo this process of spiritual death? How does the death of one man – albeit the perfect, eternal Son of God – atone for the sins of the whole world and bring those who are dead back to life? I don't know. No one really does. Not even the greatest theologian in all the world has the answer. This is the heart of the mystery of the cross. There is a profound spiritual transaction that occurs as Christ dies on the cross that we cannot truly fathom. Somehow, in the death of his perfect eternal Son, God was able to fully satisfy the spiritual judicial penalty of sin and undo its inevitable consequences. But it was, by no means an easy or a simple thing to do.

This brings us to the agony of the cross.

THE AGONY OF THE CROSS

The extent of the punishment that Christ endured on the cross cannot be underestimated. We will never fully understand the depth of his suffering – spiritual and physical – but there are glimpses of it in the descriptions of that terrible event, provided for us by the gospel writers. Matthew, Mark and Luke record Jesus' terror on the eve of his impending crucifixion, as he prayed in the garden of Gethsemane, asking the Father if there was any possible way of avoiding the horrendous events of the next day.

> " 'Father, if you are willing, take this cup from me; yet not my will but yours be done.' An angel from heaven appeared to him and strengthened him. And being in anguish, he prayed more earnestly, and his sweat was like drops of blood falling to the ground." (Luke 22:42-44)

Furthermore, Matthew and Mark record the anguished cry of Jesus as he hung, dying on the cross.

> "My God, my God, why have you forsaken me?" (Matthew 27:46 and Mark 15:34)

We need to interpret this cry of Jesus literally. As Jesus hung on the cross, he was, for the first time in eternity, utterly cut off from God the Father. God was punishing Jesus as if he had committed every sin in the world. Jesus was experiencing the full wrath of God against every act of evil that has ever been and ever will be committed. The full fury of God was being poured out upon him: the righteous anger of a holy and just God against every act of injustice and depravity and hatred and selfishness that humankind has ever committed.

As a sign of the terrible spiritual punishment that Jesus was enduring, three of the Gospel writers, Matthew, Mark and Luke, record the fact that a supernatural darkness came over the land during the crucifixion.

> "It was now about noon, and darkness came over the whole land until three in the afternoon, for the sun had stopped shining." (Luke 23:44-45)

Matthew records other extraordinary signs that took place as Jesus took his final breath:

> "At that moment the curtain of the temple was torn in two from top to bottom. The earth shook, the rocks split and the tombs broke open. The bodies of many holy people who had died were raised to life. They came out of the tombs after Jesus' resurrection and went into the holy city and appeared to many people." (Matthew 27:51-53).

Significantly, Thallus, a first century Greek historian, also wrote of this supernatural darkness and the earthquake that accompanied Christ's crucifixion. His reference was later quoted by the second century Roman historian, Sextus Julius Africanus:

> "On the whole world there pressed a fearful darkness, and the rocks were rent by an earthquake, and many places in Judea and other districts were thrown down. Thallus calls this darkness an eclipse of the sun in the third book of histories, without reason it seems to me."[1]

These astounding astronomical and geological phenomena at the time of Jesus' crucifixion signify the dreadful events that were taking place in the spiritual realm. Matthew records the fact that the people surrounding the cross who witnessed these events were *"terrified"* (Matthew 27:54). God's justice was being satisfied, judicial sentence was being carried out, sin was being punished, and the physical manifestations of that awful reality were enough to cause the first-century onlookers to step back in terror.

THE WONDER OF THE CROSS

This extraordinary sacrifice of Christ on the cross defies superlatives. It is unimaginably generous. It is inconceivably gracious. It speaks of a love that verges on the unthinkable: that a Father should allow his own Son to die for people who were living in rebellion to him.

I am a father. I have a daughter and a son. I think I am a reasonably kind and generous person – at least I try to be. But there is *no way* I would ever deliberately sacrifice the life of either of my children in order to save the life of *anyone* – even my best friend – let alone people who were my enemies. Yet this is precisely what God did:

> *"You see, at just the right time, when we were still powerless, Christ died for the ungodly. Very rarely will anyone die for a righteous person, though for a good person someone might possibly dare to die. But God demonstrates his own love for us in this: While we were still sinners, Christ died for us ... while we were God's enemies, we were reconciled to him through the death of his Son."* (Romans 5:6-10)

The cross demonstrates the wonder of God's unfathomable love for us. It is also the thing that separates Christianity from every other religion in the world. No other religion speaks of a dying deity – a god who comes to Earth to sacrifice himself for mere mortals. In fact, this concept is completely inconceivable to people in other faiths. Their gods are aloof and distant;

imperial and demanding. But Christianity teaches that the true God is not like that at all. He created us and loves us with an unimaginable love. And when we rebelled against him, he went to the most extraordinary lengths to rescue and redeem us, even to the point of dying on a cruel Roman cross.

Never doubt the love of God. The cross of Christ is its indisputable proof. When life dishes up grief and tragedy, pain and problems, such that you begin to doubt God's goodness, look to the cross. There you will see the undeniable evidence of God's amazing love for you and me.

THE ETERNAL PURPOSE OF THE CROSS

The substitutionary death of Christ for mankind is the pivotal point of human history. It is the point to which all previous history was leading and the point from which all subsequent history derives its meaning. In fact, it was God's grand plan from the beginning of eternity to send his Son to the cross in order to rescue and redeem fallen humanity. Speaking of this eternal plan of salvation, the Apostle Peter writes:

> "You were redeemed by the precious blood of Christ, a lamb without blemish or defect. <u>He was chosen before the creation of the world</u> and was revealed in these last times for your sake." (1 Peter 1:19-20)

The cross was not a last-minute adjustment to God's plans when things went unforeseeably wrong. It was not God's desperate 'Hail Mary' pass in response to unanticipated worsening circumstances. From *"before the creation of the world"* (1Peter 1:19), before any human being had been created, God knew that the cross would be necessary. In his sovereign omniscience, he foresaw that by giving us free will, we would choose to rebel against him and, in so doing, we would die spiritually.

God knew that a rescue operation would need to be mounted. And the only possible way we could be rescued was for God to take our spiritual death upon himself, at least temporarily, by Jesus dying on the cross. You see, Christ's sacrifice on the cross was already planned and decided before a single star was born, before the first sunrise on the first day, before the first human took his first breath.

This fact, in turn, reveals three further truths. Firstly, it tells us that there was no other way to save us. Surely, if there was any other way that God could have dealt with our sin and redeemed us, God would have taken it. The fact that the plan for Jesus to die on the cross was set in place from eternity, tells us that there was no other way to save us.

Secondly, it demonstrates the great value that God places upon love that is freely given. God could have avoided the cross simply by creating us with robot-like, pre-programmed obedience, without free wills capable of rebelling against him. But this would have rendered the concept of love and devotion utterly meaningless. Love only means something if it is freely given. Obedience only means something if it is freely chosen, rather than robotically pre-programmed. God so values our freely chosen love and obedience, that he was willing to pay the ultimate price, so that some might eventually choose to love and follow him of their own free wills.

Thirdly, it reveals the extreme seriousness of sin. The fact that the Son of God was predestined to die on the cross in order to pay for our sins demonstrates how dreadful and deadly sin is. If you are ever tempted to regard sin as inconsequential, if you are ever tempted to treat it lightly, just look to the cross. There is its dire consequence; there is its confronting and shocking ugliness.

. . .

THE EFFICACY OF THE CROSS

The result of this extraordinary sacrifice of Christ on the cross is the possibility of a new legal status before God for anyone who wishes it. The way has now been cleared for us to be reconciled to God. God's justice has been satisfied. The judicial sentence has been carried out. The penalty for our sins has been paid in full. Indeed, this is indicated by Christ's last word, as he took his final breath on the cross: *"tetelestai"* (τετέλεσται) – *"paid in full"* – recorded in John 19:30 (sometimes also translated *"nothing more to pay"* or *"it is finished"* in various translations).

Christ's resurrection from the dead on the following Sunday morning was the ultimate proof that our debt had been paid in full and that the way back to God was now open. Christ's crucifixion was the payment for our sin and his resurrection was the official receipt, proving that his payment was complete and sufficient. His resurrection also proves that Jesus was who he claimed to be; the eternal Son of God.

This is why the Bible declares that the resurrection of Jesus from the dead is the foundation of the Christian faith:

> *"If Christ has not been raised [from the dead], our preaching is useless and so is your faith ... and if Christ has not been raised, your faith is futile; you are still in your sins ... But Christ has indeed been raised from the dead!"* (1 Corinthians 15:14, 17, 20)

The resurrection of Christ demonstrates that the curse of spiritual death has been lifted, that the way back to God has been opened and that all who submit to Christ in faith and repentance will one day rise to eternal life as well. The resurrection of Jesus from the dead heralds the future resurrection of all who will trust in him. This is what the Bible is referring to when it says:

> "Christ has indeed been raised from the dead; the *firstfruits* of those who have fallen asleep [died]." *(1 Corinthians 15:20)*

Because of Christ's atoning sacrifice and his resurrection from the dead, the way is now opened for mankind to be reconciled to God:

> "Christ died for sins, once for all, the righteous for the unrighteous, to bring you to God." *(1 Peter 3:18)*

This is a truly stunning development. The criminal awaiting execution on death row has received an eleventh-hour pardon. Someone else has stepped in and been executed in his place. His debt has been paid, the prison cell door has been opened and he is free to go. This does not mean that this allegorical criminal is innocent. He is not. He is still guilty of the crimes he committed. But he has been pardoned. Someone else has paid for his crimes. And because of that, his death sentence has been remitted. He is set free and will henceforth be *treated* as if he is not guilty. This is what theologians refer to as *imputed righteousness*. Even though the criminal is guilty of crimes, he is now *treated* as if he had never committed them. He is gifted with an innocent status and is now able to participate in all the privileges that this new status confers upon him. He is free to re-enter society and enjoy all the benefits of unfettered citizenship.

This is the allegory that the Bible uses to describe the new legal standing before God that all who are in Christ have been granted. Our sins are paid for. Our condemnation has been removed. We have been set free to live in relationship with God as he intended.

> "Therefore, there is now no condemnation for those who are in Christ Jesus, because through Christ Jesus the law of the Spirit who gives life has set you free from the law of sin and death. For what the law was powerless to do because it was weakened by the flesh, God did by sending his own Son in the likeness of sinful flesh to be a sin offering. And so he condemned sin in the flesh." (Romans 8:1-3)

THE OUTCOME OF THE CROSS

The stunning result of Christ's sacrificial death on the cross and his resurrection from the dead is that every human being is now offered a _free_ pardon.

> "The wages of sin is death, but the _free gift_ of God is eternal life through Christ Jesus our Lord." (Romans 6:23)

This is the good news of the gospel. In fact, it is not just good news: it is great news! It is stupendous news! It is the best news possible! The way to heaven stands open, and free entry is granted to anyone who desires it. Your past can be wiped clean. A free pardon is yours for the taking.

This is what is meant by the gospel of *grace*. Salvation is not a matter of earning our way into God's favour, because that is demonstrably impossible. No one will be saved on their own merits. Salvation is only possible on the merits of Christ – what he has achieved for us through his sinless life, his perfect sacrifice on the cross and his resurrection from the dead. Salvation is a free, unmerited gift from an unimaginably generous benefactor. Salvation is by grace, and grace alone, and not through any works of our own.

> "For all have sinned and fall short of the glory of God, and are justified freely by his grace through the redemption that came by Jesus Christ." (Romans 3:23-24)

THE OFFER OF THE CROSS

The salvation that Christ has made possible is an offer only. Let me say that again. Salvation is an offer, not a universal, automatic benefit. The substitutionary death and resurrection of Jesus does not automatically save everyone. The free gift of salvation is an offer that, like all offers, must be accepted.

How we accept that offer is the topic of the next chapter, but before we leave this chapter, let me conclude by telling you a story.

David Pawson (1930 – 2020), a well-known Baptist preacher, once recounted a conversation he had with a woman on the topic of salvation. The conversation went as follows:

Pawson: *"If you died tonight and stood before God, and he asked you, 'Why should I let you into my Heaven?', what would you say to him?"*

Woman: *"I wouldn't say anything at all. I would just show him my hands."*

Pawson: *"What do you mean?"*

Woman: *"These hands have spent a lifetime serving others. I have lived for my family. I have cooked and cleaned and washed and ironed. I have cared for my husband and raised four children. I have worked tirelessly for my family. I would just hold up my hands for God to see."*

Her response is typical of the attitude we discussed in the previous chapter; the view that by our own good living we can somehow work our way into God's good books and earn a place in Heaven. But if it is possible to earn one's way into Heaven, then Jesus died in vain. If it is possible to be saved through our own good merits, Jesus did not need to go to the cross, and

God's great rescue plan, set in place from eternity past, was completely unnecessary.

Yet it was necessary. The Bible tells why it was necessary:

> "No one will be justified in God's sight by works of the law." (Romans 3:20)

> "For all have sinned and fall short of the glory of God, and are justified freely by his grace through the redemption that came by Jesus Christ." (Romans 3:23-24)

It is the cross, and the cross alone, that can save us. Only by Christ's atoning sacrifice can my sin be forgiven and my death sentence remitted.

I wonder what you would have said to that woman if it had been you she had been talking with? How would you have responded if you had been in David Pawson's shoes? Pawson recounts his reply to the woman:

> "I'm sorry, but God is not going to notice your hands. He's not even going to be looking at your hands. He'll be too busy looking at another pair of hands, nail-pierced hands, hands that were wounded for the forgiveness of your sins. And it's only by trusting in those hands that you can be right with God."

I think that's the perfect answer, don't you?

PERSONAL REFLECTION

Is there any sense in which you have not been fully trusting in the sacrifice of Christ for your salvation? Is there any way in which you have been like the woman described above, who was trusting in her own good life for her salvation? Spend some time reflecting on the extraordinary love of God for you, in allowing his Son to die so that you could be forgiven.

GROUP DISCUSSION QUESTIONS

1. Share your thoughts and impressions from this chapter. What was new to you? What was helpful? Is there anything you are still unsure about?

Read Romans 8:1-4

2. We are going to work our way backwards through this passage. Re-read the last verse and a half, from "And so he condemned sin in the flesh ..." towards the end of verse 3. This verse explains why it was necessary for Jesus to die in order to forgive us. What is the reason?

3. Why couldn't God just forgive us without allowing his Son to die? What does this teach us about the concept of divine justice?

4. Read verse 3 again. What was the 'law' powerless to do? Why?

5. Verse 3 also says that Jesus was *"in the likeness of sinful flesh"*. What do you think this means?

6. Read verses 1 – 2. What does verse 1 say that a Christian will no longer experience? Explain.

7. Verse 2 explains that a Christian is now set free from TWO things. What are they? Explain each one.

Read 1 Peter 2:21-25

8. These verses tell us what happened when Jesus died on the cross. Apart from the nails in his hands and feet, what does verse 24 tell us also happened in his body as he hung on the cross? What do you think this means?

9. Verses 24-25 tell us of TWO outcomes that Christ's sacrificial death achieved for us. What are they?

Read Romans 5:1-10

10. This passage highlights FIVE things that the death of Jesus on the cross has done for us. What are they? (TWO in verse 1 and ONE each in verses 2, 9 and 10). Explain each one.

Read Colossians 1:15-23

11. This is one of the great biblical descriptions of the person and work of Christ. Work your way through each verse, one at a time, and discuss together what each one means.

3
TRUST IN JESUS AS SAVIOUR

Jesus died and rose again to purchase our forgiveness and open the way for reconciliation with God. He is our Saviour. But his salvation doesn't automatically flow to everyone. Like the offer of a free pardon to a death-row criminal, it must be received for it to be effective. Christ's sacrifice on the cross does us no good at all unless and until we accept it for ourselves. It must be intentionally *received*, and faith is the means by which it is received:

> "God presented Christ as a sacrifice of atonement, through the shedding of his blood, to be received by faith." (Romans 3:25)

Perhaps the most succinct verse in the Bible for describing the process of salvation is found in the book of Ephesians:

> "For it is by grace you have been saved, through faith, and this not from yourselves, it is the gift of God, not by works so that no one can boast." (Ephesians 2:8-9).

This verse helps us to understand the relationship between grace, faith and good works. It is grace, and grace alone, that saves us – the grace of God made possible through the sacrifice of Christ on the cross. We are saved *by* grace. But we are saved *through* faith. Let us be clear about the distinction. Your faith does not save you; only grace can do that. Faith does not remove your sins. Only Jesus can do that. Faith is merely the means by which we *receive* God's grace. It is a bit like signing our name in order to receive an expensive parcel that someone has sent to us. Someone else paid for your gift in full and they went to the trouble of sending it to you. The delivery person knocks on your door and is ready to hand over your gift. But before you can receive it, you must sign for it. You must acknowledge that you are the intended recipient and that you are prepared to accept the parcel.

In the same way, faith is our means of acknowledging that we accept the gift that Christ is offering. More than that, it is acknowledgment of our *need* of the gift and of our complete trust in the *giver* of the gift. Faith, then, is simply us reaching out thankful arms to receive a gift we desperately need. Grace is the agent of our salvation and faith is merely our grateful response in receiving it.

Notice, too, in Ephesians 2:8, the phrase, *"and this not from yourselves, it is the gift of God"*. This is telling us that even our act of faith – our act of reaching out to receive the gift of salvation – is *"not from ourselves, it is the gift of God."* Even our faith is not something that we can dredge up from within ourselves. It is God who works within us by his Holy Spirit to stir up our faith and enable us to respond to Christ in this way. Left to our own devices, without this inner working of God's Spirit, none of us would be capable of the faith necessary to respond to God in this way; such is the sad state of our sinful, rebellious heart. Even the faith necessary to reach out to Christ is placed there by God himself. Salvation is all of God and none of me! Returning to the analogy of the parcel delivery, it is as if the giver of the gift turns up at my front door, along with the gift. Recognising that I am not even capable of signing my own name, he places the pen in my hand, enfolds my hand in his, and helps me to sign. (This, however, does not negate our free will in choosing to respond to Christ, for the scriptures are also replete with exhortations to turn to Christ in faith and repentance. More about this, shortly!)

Finally, in Ephesians 2:8-9, notice the role that good works play in the salvation process. None. Zip. The verse is very clear: *"not by works, so that no one can boast."* (I have been beating this particular drum vigorously for two chapters, so I hope the message has got through!) But this doesn't mean that God isn't concerned about how we live. The very next verse goes on to describe God's ongoing expectation for all who receive his saving grace:

> *"For we are God's handiwork, <u>created in Christ Jesus to do good works</u>, which God prepared in advance for us to do."* (Ephesians 2:10)

Once you are forgiven and saved by grace, there is a strong expectation that you will go on to live a changed life; one that is characterised by "good works". Not that these good works can save you; they are merely the grateful actions of a person who has already received God's grace and been transformed it. Indeed, it is only through the indwelling presence of Christ in your life that these good works are possible at all. This is what is meant by the phrase; *"created in Christ Jesus to do good works."*

THE NATURE OF FAITH

Having stressed that salvation is all God's work, and not mine, from beginning to end, it would be wrong to assume that we are completely passive participants in the process. If this was the case, then everyone would be saved. As with many truths in the Bible, there is a complexity to this issue which, on the surface, can seem to be contradictory. As well as declaring that it is God who causes us to have faith, the Bible also exhorts us to *have* faith. It exhorts us to turn to Christ in faith in order to be saved and it warns that those who don't respond in faith will remain under God's judgment.

We are not mere passive participants. We are called to respond. Although it is God's Spirit who stirs our hearts towards faith, we must be willing participants. God does not barge his way into every person's heart and force his gift upon them. Our spirits must work in conjunction with God's spirit. We must acquiesce to his prompting and reach out to Christ through an act of our will. We are called to *"have faith"*. For example, Jesus urged his listeners:

> *"Have faith in God."* (Mark 11:22)

This exhortation would make no sense if we were merely passive vessels into which God poured fully-formed faith. Clearly, we have a role to play in exercising faith in Christ.

So, what is the exact nature of this faith that we are exhorted to have? What is it like? True faith, saving faith, the kind of faith that God requires of you and me, has three essential elements.

1. BELIEF

At its most basic level, faith necessarily involves belief. When I sit in a chair, I am exercising faith that it will hold me up. This faith is based upon the simple belief that the chair is constructed soundly and is able to function as it was designed to – that it is, indeed, able to bear my weight.

Saving faith requires that we believe that Jesus is able to save us, that he is able to 'bear our weight'. It requires that we believe that he is who he claims to be; the risen Son of God, the Saviour of mankind who is Lord of all. Paul describes this essential basic belief in the book of Romans:

> *"If you confess with your mouth that Jesus is Lord and believe in your heart that God raised him from the dead, you will be saved."* (Romans 10:9)

The phrase *"believe in your heart"* infers not just a mental assent to these facts, but a passionate belief in them. It means being absolutely convinced that Jesus is the Saviour and, more importantly, that he is *your* Saviour. It is a deeply personal conviction.

Thus, even at this first, basic level, mere mental assent is not sufficient. True faith is more than intellectual belief in certain facts. There are plenty of people who belief that Jesus died on the cross. They may even believe that he worked miracles and rose from the dead. They may believe that he is the Son of God and the Saviour of mankind. But they have not *personalised* that belief in their hearts. They have not come to regard him as *their* Saviour. Thus, the Apostle James writes:

> *"Even the demons believe – and shudder!"* (James 2:19)

It's quite a statement isn't it. Even the devil and his demons believe that Jesus is the Son of God. In fact, they don't merely *believe* it, they *know* it – better than you and I do! They aren't stupid. Nor are they blind. They see Jesus as he really is, in the spiritual realm, more clearly than we do. They are fully aware of his divinity and his role as the Saviour of mankind. This is why, on several occasions in the Gospels, demons cried out in fear when they encountered Jesus, even acknowledging his Lordship and divinity:

> "What do you want with us, Jesus of Nazareth? Have you come to destroy us? I know who you are—the Holy One of God!" (Luke 4:34)

The point is, demons believe all the right 'stuff' about Jesus; they know who he is, but they aren't saved because they are living in rebellion to Jesus. They know he is the Saviour, but they have not *acted* on that belief to make him *their* Saviour.

Which brings me to the next key element.

2. TRUST

In the case of a chair, I am not truly exercising faith in it until I sit on it and trust my weight to it. I can stand beside the chair and acknowledge how well it has been made, I can praise the strength of its joints and the integrity of its design, but until I sit in the chair, I am not exercising faith; I simply have belief. Faith means placing your *trust* in the object of your belief. Jesus said:

> "Trust in God; trust also in me" (John 14:1)

The Bible word used in that verse, "*pisteuo*" (πιστεύω) means more than mere intellectual belief – it means an active *trust* in that belief. Jesus calls us to not merely *believe* that he is the Saviour, but to *trust* him as our Saviour. He calls us to not merely *believe* that he can wipe away our sins, but to *trust* that he has done so. And if we are to truly trust Jesus in this way, we must stop trusting in ourselves. We must transfer the trust for our salvation from our own hands into the hands of the only

One who *can* save us. We must give up our pitiful attempts to earn forgiveness through our own ill-perceived self-righteousness, and place our trust completely in the atoning sacrifice of Christ on the cross for our sins.

The context of Jesus' statement in John 14:1 is significant. His exhortation to, *"trust in God; trust also in me,"* is the prelude to his assurance that he is able to take us safely to Heaven. The full passage reads:

> *"Do not let your hearts be troubled. Trust in God; trust also in me. My Father's house has many rooms; if that were not so, would I have told you that I am going there to prepare a place for you? And if I go and prepare a place for you, I will come back and take you to be with me that you also may be where I am." (John 14:1-3)*

Jesus is not merely asking us to trust him to solve our little problems in life. He is not calling us to trust him for healing or financial help or relationship guidance. No. These things pale into insignificance compared to what Jesus is asking trust for. He is asking us to trust him for the biggest thing of all; for our eternal salvation. He is asking us to trust that he will safely deliver us into our eternal home.

It is this kind of 'big trust' that characterises the true Christian. The Christian is someone who has placed their trust completely and utterly in Jesus for their salvation and has ceased their ineffective striving for self-justification. They have come to rest completely in Jesus as the sole means of their salvation.

3. REPENTANCE: COMMITMENT TO JESUS' LORDSHIP

This is the third vital element of saving faith. I will have much more to say about this in the next chapter, but for the moment, it is vital to understand that faith is an active thing, not passive.

True faith, saving faith, must involve a transformed life – a commitment to begin to live under the Lordship of Christ. It involves beginning to live as if you really *believe* that Jesus is Lord. The person who bows his knee and says to Jesus, *"You are my Lord,"* but then walks off and continues to flagrantly and consistently disobey him has not transferred belief into action. It is not true faith, but mere belief. This kind of shallow, intellectual assent is what prompted Jesus, on one occasion, to lament:

> "Why do you call me, 'Lord, Lord', when you don't do what I tell you?" (Luke 6:46)

As we shall see in the next chapter, this does not infer perfect obedience, for that will never happen. We will remain imperfect sinners in need of forgiveness until the day we die. But it does mean a determined commitment to begin to live under Christ's rule. It means a strong desire to begin to honour God with our lives and serve Christ as our new Master.

THE DECISION OF FAITH

Saving faith involves the three essential elements of belief, trust and an ongoing commitment to Christ as Lord (repentance). It is this kind of faith that is essential in order to be saved. You cannot be saved without it.

But this requires a decision of the will. God's Spirit can only stir your heart and convict you up to a certain point. As I said before, God is not going to forcibly barge his way into your heart. In the book of Revelation, Jesus sends a message to people living in the city of Laodicea:

> *"Here I am! I stand at the door and knock. If anyone hears my voice and opens the door, I will come in and eat with that person, and they with me." (Revelation 3:20)*

The reference to 'eating' infers an intimate, personal friendship – one where whatever barrier may have been in place previously has been removed. If we are willing to open the door of our heart, the God who was once distant and removed from us, promises to actually make his home *within* us. It is an extraordinary offer! Although this invitation was originally written to members of a church who had strayed from their original fellowship with Jesus, (in fact, they had strayed so far that Jesus is now standing outside the door to their hearts again), it is equally applicable to anyone who is currently not in close relationship with God.

This verse demonstrates a vital concept in our understanding of salvation. God knocks on the door of our heart, but we must open the door. A response of faith towards Jesus requires an intentional act of our will. We must choose to either accept Christ's offer of grace or reject it.

Let us revisit the allegory of a condemned criminal on death row, that I spoke about in the previous chapter. Christ unlocks the cell door, but does not go in. He stands outside the cell, looking in. He then offers the criminal a free pardon, written by God himself and signed in Jesus' own blood. He holds the signed pardon through the bars of the cell for the criminal to see. All the criminal needs to do is humble himself and receive it with a grateful, penitent heart. He simply needs to reach out and take hold of the free pardon, open the unlocked cell door and walk free. It would be utterly foolish for him to reject it, would it not? It would be folly of the highest order if he refused to leave his cell. Yet this is what many people do in regard to the free pardon that Christ offers.

Two centuries ago, there was an extraordinary case of a man who literally refused a death row pardon. In 1833, George Wilson was convicted of robbing the U.S. Mail in Pennsylvania and was sentenced to death. His many friends advocated for him and petitioned the government. Finally, President Andrew Jackson granted Wilson a presidential pardon. However, in an unprecedented and extraordinary turn of events, George Wilson refused to accept the pardon. His guards and friends and legal councillors all pleaded with him, showing him the signed presidential pardon, to no avail. Wilson was adamant that he did not want to be pardoned. This unprecedented situation created much confusion within the legal system. No one knew what to do. Eventually, the case was taken to the Supreme Court which, after much deliberation, delivered the following verdict:

> "A pardon is a deed, to the validity of which, delivery is essential, and delivery is not complete without acceptance. It may then be rejected by the person to whom it is tendered; and if it is rejected, we have discovered no power in this court to force it upon him." [1]

In other words, *a pardon is only valid if it is accepted*. George Wilson was eventually hanged, simply because of his obstinate refusal to accept a free pardon.

As difficult to believe as that example is (and I assure you, it is factual), this is precisely what is occurring all over our world today in regard to Christ's offer of salvation. The penalty for sin has been paid and a free pardon is held out to all mankind. Christ stands at the door to our prison cell and holds out a pardon written in his blood and signed by his Father. All we need to do is accept the free gift, by accepting the giver himself – Jesus Christ, our Lord and Saviour. But, tragically, almost unbelievably, many people refuse. And because they refuse, the pardon is forfeited and their sentence must be carried out, just as it was in the case of George Wilson.

Why would anyone reject Christ's offer of a free pardon? There are really only two reasons: pride and unbelief.

Pride

The proud are convinced that they can do it themselves. *"I've lived a good life. I'm a good person. I've done enough for God to let me into heaven."* Such a person has no comprehension of the depth of their own sinfulness and how impossibly short of God's standards they fall. I dealt with this false belief in great detail in the first chapter.

Unbelief

Unbelief is the other reason people refuse Christ's offer of salvation. Many don't believe that Jesus is who he said he was - the Son of God, the Lord of mankind and the Saviour of the world. They refuse to believe the overwhelming evidence of his miracles, as recorded by verifiable historical documents. They refuse to believe that there is anything beyond the grave. They refuse to accept the message of the Bible and choose, instead, to believe the myth of a godless universe and a meaningless existence.

The Bible indicates that this kind of unbelief is a key factor in people being separated from God for eternity. In the book of Roman, Paul laments the fact that many Jews have missed out on salvation and *"were broken off* [separated from God] *because of unbelief."* (Romans 11:20). Similarly, in the book of Hebrews we find a warning, *"do not harden your hearts"* because those who did so in the past *"were not able to enter* [God's presence] *because of their unbelief."* (Hebrews 3:15 and 19). Indeed, those who disbelieve and reject the truth cannot be saved:

> "Whoever <u>believes</u> in the Son has eternal life. But whoever <u>rejects</u> the Son will not see life, for God's wrath remains on them." (John 3:36)

The sad fact is that there will be many people who will end up separated from God eternally and will experience his wrath for their sins, not because they are worse sinners that you or I, but simply because of their pride and unbelief. They refuse to exercise faith in Christ.

TWO CONTRASTING RESPONSES

The Gospel writers describe two criminals who were crucified alongside Jesus on the hill called Golgotha and record their two very different responses to Jesus. Their responses are an allegory of the two distinct responses toward Jesus that people continue to make today. One criminal demonstrated unbelief and pride, hurling insults at Jesus and ridiculing him, refusing to believe that he was who he claimed to be. The other criminal responded very differently. He began by rebuking the first criminal:

> "Don't you fear God, since we are under the same sentence? We are punished justly, for we are getting what our sins deserve, but this man has done nothing wrong." (Luke 23:40-41).

This is a frank admission. He must have done some very bad things if he admits that both he and the other criminal deserve to die. Make no mistake about it, these two criminals were very bad people! But then this second criminal turned to Jesus and responded completely unexpectedly:

> "Jesus, remember me when you come into your kingdom." (Luke 23:42)

In responding as he did, this second criminal expressed a simple faith in Jesus as the coming King, admitting his own guilt and asking for mercy.

Then we come to the most surprising, indeed shocking, part of this whole incident. To this second criminal, Jesus responded:

> *"Truly, I say to you, today you will be with me in paradise."* (Luke 23:43)

What an astonishing statement! Jesus was effectively saying that this self-confessed criminal, who by his own admission had committed such serious crimes that he deserved to die, would be granted a free pass into Heaven! How could Jesus allow such a self-confessed 'baddie' into God's paradise? How could Jesus overlook the terrible things that this man must have done? The answer is that Jesus **didn't** overlook this man's sin. Instead, he paid the price for it himself. Even as they were having this conversation, Jesus was dying for that man's sin. He was paying the penalty for the man's wrongdoing, so that people like him, and people like me and you, can be forgiven.

And did you notice what that forgiven criminal did NOT have a chance to do? He didn't have a chance to turn over a new leaf. He didn't have a chance to lift his game, to clean up his act, to stop doing bad things and to make himself more acceptable to God. All he could do was continue to hang there, dying. He was not able to offer up a SINGLE THING toward his own salvation. He could only do one thing, the only thing that any of us can do: he threw himself on the mercy of Jesus, acknowledging Jesus as his rightful King and trusting in Jesus for his forgiveness. That's it! Nothing else! And that is precisely what everyone must do in order to be saved.

You see, salvation is all about God's grace, freely given, undeserved and unmerited. We bring nothing to the table. Our hands are empty. In fact, they must be empty, because it is only when they are empty that we can reach out and receive. They must be empty of any and all things that we would hold up to God, saying *"Look what I have done! Look how good I am! Look at my achievements! Look at my good life! Surely I deserve eternal life!"* God turns aside from people with full hands and proud hearts, for he sees their achievements for what they are: pitifully inadequate offerings, tainted by pride and completely inadequate in their inability to atone for the vast record of their sinfulness.

> *"For it is by grace you are saved, through faith, and this not from yourselves, it is the gift of God, <u>not by works, so that no one can boast</u>." (Ephesians 2:8-9)*

What about you? What are you holding in your hands? What are you trusting in for your salvation? Are you trusting in your own good works? Are you trusting in the record of your good service; your years of charity work or your dedicated service in your local church? Is that what is in your hands? Is that what you are holding up to God, saying, *"Look what I have done. Surely, this is good enough?"*

If that is the case, you must empty your hands immediately. Right now. Without another moment's hesitation. Those things cannot save you. Only Jesus can. You need the grace of the Saviour. But you can't receive his grace while your hands are full of your own self-righteousness. You must lay those things down. You must cease trusting in your own goodness, and trust fully and only in the grace of Jesus. You must reach out with empty hands and a humble, penitent heart, asking for his mercy and trusting in his goodness.

You must place your faith in Christ, and Christ alone.

If you would like to make this step of faith, don't put it off. Do it now, while the Spirit of God is working in your heart. Here is a simple prayer you might like to pray:

> *"Dear God, I confess that I am a sinner who has fallen hopelessly short of your perfect standards. I sin in thought, word and deed, deliberately doing what I know to be wrong and failing to do what I know to be right. Please forgive me, not only for these individual sins, but also for the sin of my self-reliance. Lord Jesus, I believe you are the Son of God. I believe you died on the cross to forgive my sins and rose from the dead to be declared Lord of all. I trust you now as my Saviour and I humbly ask for your mercy. I open my heart to you and ask that you will come into my life. Please fill me with Your presence and strengthen me to follow you all the days of my life. Amen."*

If you prayed that prayer humbly and sincerely, whether for the first time or the 100th time, then you have done all that God requires for you to be forgiven. You are a child of God, who has crossed over from death to life, from condemnation to forgiveness, and there is a place in heaven for you. The prison door has swung wide and you have walked through it, holding onto a free pardon written in the blood of the Saviour. You have been saved by grace, through faith.

∽

PERSONAL REFLECTION

Have you responded to Jesus Christ with humble and heartfelt faith and repentance? Did you pray that prayer at the end of the chapter? Even for people who have been Christians for decades, it does us good to again commit ourselves to Christ in simple faith and repentance. If you didn't already do so, perhaps you might like to pray through that prayer, refreshing your commitment to Christ as your Saviour and Lord.

Upon reflection, do you think you have completely understood the gospel up to this point in your life? In what ways has this chapter helped refine your understanding of the gospel? Are there subtle emphases which have become clearer to you? Is there any sense in which you have been trusting in your own good works and religious service rather than the work of Christ for your salvation?

GROUP DISCUSSION QUESTIONS

1. Share your thoughts and impressions from this chapter. What was new to you? What was helpful? Is there anything you are still unsure about?

Read Romans 3:9-20

2. This passage describes our total inability to save ourselves. (We have already covered this in previous chapters, but it is worth briefly revisiting it). In particular, note verses 10 and 20. What are these two verses saying?

Read the next section: Romans 3:21-26. (Here comes the cavalry!)

3. How would you summarise this passage in your own words?

4. What is the only way we can be declared "righteous"? (verse 22).

5. Who are the only ones who will be justified by God? (verse 26).

Read Ephesians 2:1-10

6. Verse 8 explains that we are saved BY grace, THROUGH faith. Explain the significant differences between these two

words, "by" and "through". Why would it be unhelpful to say that we are saved "by" faith?

7. Verse 9 explains the role that good works plays in our salvation. What is it?

8. Read verse 10 and note the reference to "good works". Although good works cannot save us, what does this verse tell us about their role in the Christian life? How are they linked to faith?

Read John 14:1-3

9. Why do you think Jesus starts by saying, *"Do not let your hearts be troubled"*? What kind of worry or anxiety is he particularly speaking about in this passage? What, in particular, is Jesus asking us to trust him about in this passage? (see verse 3).

Read Hebrews 11:1-16

10. Verse 1 provides us with a wonderful definition of faith. How does this definition differentiate true faith from mere wishful thinking?

11. Notice the 'future focus' aspect of faith, outlined in verses 13-16. In particular, what similarity is there between verse 16 and the previous passage we examined in John 14:1-3?

12. If we have a strong 'future focus' in our faith, how should this change the way we live now? (see the end of verse 13).

4
SUBMIT TO JESUS AS LORD

In the previous chapter we examined how a person becomes connected with God by an act of undeserved grace which is received through faith in Jesus. But there is a vital concept that must go hand in hand with this, if we are to maintain and deepen our connection with God. It is the concept of repentance. Repentance is not an 'add on' to faith, it describes the practical *outworking* of our faith, and it is essential if our faith is to be proved genuine. Sadly, this is a poorly taught and commonly misunderstood concept in many churches today, and it has been de-emphasised in modern preaching.

The Scriptures are replete with references to the essential nature of repentance for salvation:

> "Repent, for the kingdom of heaven is at hand." (Matthew 3:2)

> "Repent, for the kingdom of heaven has come near." (Matthew 4:17)

> "Then Jesus began to denounce the towns in which most of his miracles had been performed, because they did not repent." (Matthew 11:20)

> "After John was put in prison, Jesus went into Galilee, proclaiming the good news of God. 'The kingdom of God is at hand. Repent and believe the good news!'" (Mark 1:14-15)
>
> "Jesus answered ... 'Unless you repent, you too will perish!'" (Luke 13:2 and again in verse 5)
>
> "I tell you that there will be more rejoicing in heaven over one sinner who repents than over ninety-nine righteous persons who do not need to repent." (Luke 15:7)
>
> "Peter replied, 'Repent and be baptised, every one of you, in the name of Jesus Christ for the forgiveness of your sins." (Acts 2:38)
>
> "Repent and turn to God, so that your sins may be wiped out and times of refreshing may come from the Lord" (Acts 3:19)
>
> "In the past, God overlooked such ignorance, but now he commands all people everywhere to repent." (Acts 17:30)
>
> "I preached that they should repent and turn to God and demonstrate their repentance by their deeds." (Acts 26:20)

Repentance is an essential component of one's faith-response to Christ. This is why Jesus and the Apostles constantly demanded it of people. But what does it actually mean?

The Bible word for 'repent' is "*metanoeo*" (μετανοέω). It means a radical change of direction; doing a 'U-turn'.

In the first century, a Roman soldier who encountered a Jew who was walking on the same road but travelling in the opposite direction had the Emperor's authority to command that Jew to "metanoeo" – to turn around and walk beside the soldier and carry his pack for 1,000 paces (one kilometre). It sounds very harsh, and was often extremely inconvenient for the Jew, who was then forced to retrace his steps, adding an additional two kilometres to his journey. (Imagine how frustrated that Jew might be if he then encountered a second Roman soldier!).

The Bible says that mankind is walking in the opposite direction to God. We have all turned our backs on him and "turned to our own way":

> "We all like sheep have gone astray; all of us have turned to our own way." (Isaiah 53:6)

This is called sin, and at its heart, it is a resolute determination to live life *our* way and not God's.

However, when we place our faith in Christ, he commands us to turn around, to do a "U-turn" and walk beside him. He commands us to 'metanoeo'. There are three important differences between Christ's call to 'metanoeo' and that of the Roman soldier.

Firstly, Jesus does not call us to walk beside him for a mere 1,000 steps. It is a life-long call. This might seem very demanding, but it is not at all, particularly when you consider the next two elements of his call.

Secondly, he does not weigh us down harshly. The Roman soldier's pack could weigh up to 100 pounds (45 kilograms). In Jesus' case, he promises:

> "Come to me, all you who are weary and burdened, and I will give you rest. Take my yoke upon you and learn from me, for I am gentle and humble of heart; and you will find rest. For my yoke is easy, and my burden is light." (Matthew 11:28-30)

This is a subtle reference to the enforced carrying of a Roman soldier's pack in the first century. Jesus' listeners would have understood this implicitly. Jesus is assuring us that, unlike the heavy pack of the Roman soldier, the 'yoke' he asks us to wear will not be burdensome. But, nonetheless, there *is* a yoke. It is the yoke that ties us to him as our new Lord. It is the yoke of our pledged obedience to him. Jesus asks that we make a commitment to obey him now, as our new Master. While this might seem daunting, Jesus promises that if we truly open our hearts to him as Lord and Saviour *"my yoke is easy and my burden is light"* (Matthew 11:30). That is because we do not have to attempt to obey him in our own strength, for his indwelling Spirit will strengthen and empower us to do so joyfully.

Thirdly, in comparison to the Roman soldier who has a purely selfish and heartless motivation in compelling a Jew to 'metanoeo', Jesus' call for us to turn and walk beside him is for *our* benefit, not his. In the verse quoted above, he says to us:

> *"Come to me all who are weary and burdened and I will give you rest."* (Matthew 11:28)

Jesus sees that we are walking in the wrong direction, and that the path we have chosen is self-destructive and burdensome. He calls us to a better life; the life we were created to live, a life in loving relationship with the God who made us, who loves us and knows what is best for us.

> *"I have come to give you life; life in all its fullness"* (John 10:10)

This all sounds very appealing, doesn't it? But there is a cost involved. We must turn from the way we were living. We must radically change our direction. It is not a subtle course alteration that Jesus demands of us. Repentance involves doing a complete 'U-turn'. In essence, it involves relinquishing control of your life to Jesus.

Back in the 1980s, when I was driving my first car (a Datsun 1200), I used to occasionally pick up hitchhikers. Hitchhiking was more of an accepted "thing" back then. I used to enjoy meeting all sorts of interesting people and chatting to them.

A lot of people think that becoming a Christian and 'inviting Jesus into your life' is like picking up a hitchhiker. Let me explain.

Imagine you are driving your car along a highway and you come across Jesus standing by the side of the road, hitchhiking. You pull your car over to the side of the road and stop beside him. You wind down your passenger window and lean across, asking, "Would you like a lift?" Jesus replies, "*You need to let me in.*" You find this response slightly puzzling, but you let it slide. You ask, "Where are you headed? Are you going my way?". Jesus replies, "*I am going my way, not yours, and you need to come with me.*" Again, you find this puzzling, but you decide not to question him further. You lean across and open the passenger door, saying, "OK. Hop in!".

But Jesus does a curious thing. Instead of getting into your car, he closes the passenger door and walks around the front of the car until he is standing at your driver's door. He opens your door, leans in and says, "*Move over. I'm doing the driving from now on.*" Now you are perplexed. "But it's my car!" you complain. Jesus merely responds, "*Unless you let me do the driving, I will not enter your car. I am not here to be a passenger.*"

At this point you have a decision to make. *Do I keep driving the car myself, or do I let Jesus take control?* Something about Jesus prompts you to submit. You slide across to the passenger side and Jesus sits behind the wheel. Immediately, he executes a U-turn and starts driving back the way you had come. You complain, "Hey! That's not the way I was going!" Jesus responds, "*I know. You were going the wrong way.*"

This is what it means to respond to Jesus in faith and repentance. Faith means trusting that Jesus is who he says he is – the Saviour who can take us to Heaven – and repentance is the act of handing the steering wheel of our life over to him. Can you see how the two things go together? In fact, can you see how inseparable they are? You can't truly say to Jesus, *"I trust you as my Saviour"* but then refuse to hand the steering wheel of your life over to him. If you aren't letting Jesus do the driving, if you aren't obeying him as your new Master, you really haven't trusted him as your Saviour.

You can't pick up Jesus like you would a hitchhiker. He doesn't enter your life as a passive passenger. He gets to do the driving now, not you. He gets to determine the direction of our life. He gets to determine your morals and ethics. Jesus either comes into your life as Lord of all or he doesn't come in at all.

A lot of people have stopped their "car" by the side of the road and invited Jesus to come in, but they are still doing the driving. They have continued on down the road, travelling in the same direction that they were travelling in before, with themselves still in control. They are still deciding their own morality. They are still disobeying some of Christ's clear commands. But they are in for a rude shock! Because Jesus is not in their car. They think he is; after all, they invited him in! But Jesus is still back on the side of the road. He did not get into their car, because they refused to relinquish the steering wheel to him. Jesus refuses to be a passive passenger.

Sadly, there will be many people on the Day of Judgment who believe they are Christians, who have 'asked Jesus into their heart', but who will be condemned by Christ because they did not submit to him as Lord.

"Not everyone who says to me, 'Lord, Lord,' will enter the kingdom of heaven, but only the one who does the will of my Father who is in heaven. Many will say to me on that day, 'Lord, Lord, did we not prophesy in your name and in your name drive out demons and, in your name, perform many miracles?' Then I will tell them plainly, 'I never knew you. Away from me, you evildoers!'" (Matthew 7:21-23)

A SHOCKING PARABLE

One of the most important passages in the whole Bible for our understanding of repentance is a parable that Jesus told to his disciples, recorded for us in Matthew 18. It is such a crucial passage of scripture, that it is worth quoting here in full.

"Therefore, the kingdom of heaven is like a king who wanted to settle accounts with his servants. ^{24} As he began the settlement, a man who owed him ten thousand bags of gold was brought to him. ^{25} Since he was not able to pay, the master ordered that he and his wife and his children and all that he had be sold to repay the debt. ^{26} "At this the servant fell on his knees before him. 'Be patient with me,' he begged, 'and I will pay back everything.' ^{27} The servant's master took pity on him, cancelled the debt and let him go. ^{28} "But when that servant went out, he found one of his fellow servants who owed him a hundred silver coins. He grabbed him and began to choke him. 'Pay back what you owe me!' he demanded. ^{29} "His fellow servant fell to his knees and begged him, 'Be patient with me, and I will pay it back.' ^{30} "But he refused. Instead, he went off and had the man thrown into prison until he could pay the debt. ^{31} When the other servants saw what had happened, they were outraged and went and told their master everything that had happened. ^{32} "Then the master called the servant in. 'You wicked servant,' he said, 'I cancelled all that debt of yours because you begged me to. ^{33} Shouldn't you have had mercy on your fellow servant just as I had

on you?' ³⁴ In anger his master handed him over to the jailers to be tortured, until he should pay back all he owed. ³⁵ "This is how my heavenly Father will treat each of you unless you forgive your brother or sister from your heart." (Matthew 18:23-35)

This is a parable about grace. Grace that is undeserved and unmerited. Grace that is bestowed upon a hopelessly indebted servant by a merciful and benevolent King. But let us unpack the parable in greater detail.

The first thing to note is that the servant's debt was huge: ten thousand bags of gold. In today's dollars, that's roughly 320 million dollars. This man's debt was astronomical! That servant could work his entire life and never come close to repaying such a debt.

Jesus is very deliberate in depicting such an impossibly huge debt. He is making a very important point here. That servant represents you and me. He represents every human being's position in regard to their standing before a holy God. Each of us, over our lifetime, accumulates such an astronomically large debt of sin that it is impossible for any of us to "pay it off". We examined this concept in detail in the first chapter.

The second important concept illustrated by the parable should be equally familiar: the extraordinarily generous nature of God's forgiveness. The King in this parable forgives the servant of his debt of ten thousand bags of gold. He completely wipes the debt. The servant is released with nothing further to pay. He is not put on a future payment plan. His future wages are not garnisheed. He doesn't have to do a zillion hours of community service to pay off his debt. He is simply released, and his past debt is completely wiped clean. It is an incredibly generous gift that he is given.

This is grace, and it is given to him freely. It is unmerited. It is undeserved. It is unexpected. This is what we mean when we say that grace is free. But let us be clear about what we mean by this word, "free". Because, in the parable, it cost the King thirty-two million dollars to pardon the servant. It was free to the servant but not to the King: it cost him dearly. The King effectively paid ten thousand bags of gold himself to free the servant from his debt.

In God's case, it cost him even more to offer us a free pardon. It cost him the death of his Son to forgive us our sins. The grace that comes freely to us, comes at a great price to God.

To this point, this parable told by Jesus to his disciples has followed a familiar discourse – at least one that is familiar to most Christians within the modern church. But the parable is about to take a surprising, even shocking, turn. It's a twist that we would not expect at all. Certainly not from the lips of a loving, forgiving Saviour.

When the servant is forgiven his debt and set free from prison, the first thing he does is he goes out and finds someone who owes him a couple of hundred dollars and demands payment. When the debtor asks for mercy and for more time to pay, the servant refuses and throws the debtor into prison. Upon hearing of this, the King orders the servant to be re-arrested. The servant is then brought before the King again, and the King is furious. He says to the servant:

> 'You wicked servant! I cancelled all that debt of yours because you begged me to. [33] Shouldn't you have had mercy on your fellow servant just as I had on you?' [34] In anger his master handed him over to the jailers to be tortured, until he should pay back all he owed. [35] "This is how my heavenly Father will treat each of you

unless you forgive your brother or sister from your heart." (Matthew 18:32-35)

Do you see what has happened here? The servant's original forgiveness is rescinded. The grace that was originally given to him is now withdrawn. The debt that was originally cancelled is now reinstated. And the punishment that was originally waved is now fully enforced once more. Or, to put it into Christian parlance, the sinner who was once saved is no longer saved.

I can already see your hackles rising. I can sense your upwelling of protestation. I can already hear you beginning to chant: "once saved, always saved." Now is not the time for a discussion of that belief, although if you're interested, the last chapter of my book, *"Rethinking the Gospel: Challenging the Modern Misconception",* deals with that popular misconception in detail.

Leaving that more complex issue aside, however, let us be crystal clear what has happened in this instance. The servant was once the recipient of grace, but that grace has now been rescinded. And the vital question is: "WHY?" What was the great sin that the servant committed that caused the loss of the King's grace? Surely one single sin, one single act of unforgiveness, can't be responsible? Because if that's the case, then we are all doomed!

No. This parable can't be inferring that in order to remain saved a person must never sin again. To go down this path would be to lead us to the false doctrine of salvation by works. Just as one's initial reception of salvation is by grace alone, so is its ongoing retention. Salvation is by God's grace, from beginning to end. It is, and always will be, an undeserved gift. We never reach a point where we merit or deserve salvation because of our good living or our perfect obedience to God. We live our Christian lives at the foot of the cross, needing Christ's forgiveness daily. Indeed, 1 John 1:8-10 explicitly describes this ongoing, daily need of the Christian to be forgiven for his or her failings:

> "If we claim to be without sin, we deceive ourselves and the truth is not in us. If we confess our sins, he is faithful and just and will forgive us our sins and purify us from all unrighteousness. If we claim we have not sinned, we make him out to be a liar and his word is not in us." (1 John 1:8-10)

The verse immediately preceding this, states:

> "... the blood of Jesus, God's Son, <u>purifies</u> us from all sin" (1 John 1:7)

The verb, "<u>purifies</u>" (katharizo) in this verse is written in the present imperative tense, indicating that it is an ongoing process rather than a single event at one's conversion. In other words, we will remain in continual need of Christ's forgiveness every day of our lives. We will never be perfect in this life.

So, given that perfection is not required in order to remain saved, (otherwise no one would be saved!), what was it that caused the servant in the parable to have his forgiveness rescinded and his punishment reinstated?

It was more than just a single sin – a single instance of unforgiveness. There was something FUNDAMENTALLY MISSING from the servant's response to his master: something so serious that he forfeited the grace that was initially given to him.

The answer is that he was not transformed by the grace he received. He refused to extend the same grace to others and, by not doing so, he revealed that there was a critical element missing in his response to the King's grace.

Now we come to the crucial heart of the issue; one that is very poorly understood by many Christians. The King's grace was given to the servant freely and undeservedly, but it was not unconditional. Let me say that again. Grace is free, but it is not unconditional. There is an important distinction. In the case of the parable, the King clearly required that the servant should begin to show others the same mercy that he had received. The King expected the servant to go forth and live a transformed life – a life transformed from the inside out by the undeserved grace he had been given. This expectation of the King is not explicitly iterated in the first half of the parable, but it is abundantly evident in the latter half, when we see the King's fury at the servant's lack of grace. Grace was given, but it came laden with an expectation; a *condition*. It was given freely and undeservedly, but its ongoing retention was **conditional** upon a major change in the life of the recipient; a response that was required.

The problem with the unforgiving servant in the parable was not an individual act of unforgiveness. The servant's lack of forgiveness was merely indicative of a deeper, more fundamental problem: he had not been transformed by his encounter with the King's grace. His reception of grace had left him relieved of his debt but unchanged in his heart. He arose and walked out of the King's presence essentially the same man as when he was arrested. He was unchanged. He was still greedy and conniving and unforgiving. There was no *repentance*. And that lack of repentance demonstrated his lack of appreciation for the gift he had received. He cheapened the gift, treating it off-handedly, as if it had no real consequence for his ongoing behaviour. He dishonoured the gift he had been given and, by so doing, dishonoured the King who gave it.

GRACE IS FREE BUT CONDITIONAL

Let me reiterate a crucial point: grace is free, but it is not unconditional. If grace was unconditional, then everyone would be saved. Let me say that again: **if grace was unconditional, then everyone on earth would be saved.** The fact that not everyone is saved tells us that there are *conditions* that must be met in order to receive God's grace. In fact, there are two conditions, and they are two sides of the one coin; faith and repentance. Grace is free, but it is not given to everyone. It is only given to those who respond to God in faith and repentance. Those are the two conditions. Grace is the gift; faith and repentance is the means of receiving it.

Furthermore, the Bible teaches that you cannot have true faith without repentance. If there is no genuine repentance, no changing of behaviour to henceforth live under the Lordship of Christ, it is just belief that a person is displaying and not true faith. This, in fact, is the key message of the whole book of James. Consider some of these statements:

> *"Faith by itself, if it is not accompanied by action, is dead"* (James 2:17)

> *"Faith without deeds is useless"* (James 2:20)

> *"A person is considered righteous by what they do, and not by faith alone."* (James 2:24)

> *"As the body without the spirit is dead, so faith without deeds is dead"* (James 2:26)

Reading through these and other verses in the book of James, it is easy to see how some people can regard these statements as contradicting the message of salvation by grace through faith, found elsewhere in the New Testament. On the surface, these verses in James almost seem to be promoting good works as a means of salvation, saying that faith is not enough. The misinterpretation that many people make is one of semantics. James is not attempting to ADD repentance or good deeds to faith; he is DEFINING faith. Faith, if it is genuine, will always result in a changed life. The inner enthronement of Christ in one's heart will give birth to an outer transformation. It is inevitable. It is inescapable.

Jesus speaks of this inextricable link between faith and repentance:

> "If you love me, you will obey my commandments." (John 14:15)

> "Anyone who loves me will obey my teaching." (John 14:23)

The Apostle John also came to understand this inseparable link:

> "We know that we have come to know him if we keep his commands. Whoever says, "I know him," but does not do what he commands is a liar, and the truth is not in that person." (1 John 2:3-4)

Similarly, the Apostle Paul, champion of the doctrine of salvation by grace alone through faith alone, also wrote of the essential nature of ongoing repentance:

> "God will repay each person according to what they have done. To those who by persistence in doing good seek glory, honour and immortality, he will give eternal life. But for those who are self-seeking and who reject the truth and follow evil, there will be wrath and anger." (Romans 2:6-8)

Paul is not contradicting his continual emphasis that people are saved not by their own works but by faith in Christ. He is simply declaring that *"persistence in doing good"* is a key element of saving faith and is, in fact, the proof of its genuine nature.

We must ensure that we have a biblical theology of salvation. A person cannot be saved without genuine, heart-felt repentance and a commitment to obey Christ as Lord. Once again, let me reiterate, this does not infer that a true Christian will never sin. We will continue to fall far short of God's perfect standard. But repentance means that our hearts and lives are now heading in a new direction; one that will be inevitably and abundantly evident from our transformed behaviour and attitudes. It cannot be otherwise. If this is not the case, then we have not truly come to know Christ.

A PERSONAL CHALLENGE

A discussion of the biblical necessity of repentance demands that we pause for self-examination. Have you truly repented? Has your faith in Christ resulted in an obvious change in your behaviour and attitudes? Have you begun to live under Christ's Lordship, seeking to obey him now and turn from your past sinful patterns? Has your faith in Christ and your encounter with the message of God's grace actually transformed you?

Or are you essentially unchanged? Are you still mastered by your old sinful habits? Do you still cling to unhealthy patterns of behaviour? Have you refused to let go of them? Are you still doing the 'driving'?

If you have not repented and made a fresh start, turning to obey Christ as your Lord, then whatever it is you think you have, it is not faith. It is mere belief. Like the demons who believe in Jesus but do not submit to him, you are an unrepentant believer, not a Christian. And Jesus would say to you, as he said to unrepentant believers two millennia ago"

> "Why do you call me 'Lord, Lord' and do not do the things I say?" (Luke 6:46)

Let me get very specific:

- Are you addicted to pornography?
- Are you involved in adulterous or illicit sexual relationships?
- Are you having sex with your boyfriend or girlfriend?
- Are you a perpetual liar?
- Are you a perpetual gossip and slanderer?
- Do you regularly engage in dirty, smutty jokes?
- Are you a constantly bitter, unforgiving person?
- Are you constantly negative and critical, seeking to tear others down and build yourself up?
- Are you ruled by pride and selfishness?

These are not the marks of a repentant Christian. These are not the characteristics of someone who has come to know Christ and been transformed by his grace. You cannot truly claim to be a Christian, a follower of Christ, while clearly not following him. If your life continues to be characterised by these blatant and habitual kinds of sin, with no serious effort or desire to turn from them, then you have not repented. You are an unrepentant believer, not a Christian. You do not have faith; you simply have belief. Because true faith is demonstrated by repentance.

Sadly, there are some people within the institutional church who are in this category. Sunday pews contain some hand-waving, hymn-singing believers who give every appearance of being born again Christians, yet their lives beyond the church doors indicate that they are not really following Christ at all. They are not obeying him. There are even ministers, pastors and priests in this category, whose hypocrisy is sometimes publicly brought to light. They put on a good Sunday show. They are good at what they do. They can preach a good message, they can hold a crowd, they use all the right words. They may have a large social media following. They are accomplished at presenting an impressive spiritual façade. But their conduct throughout the week is not infused with the grace of Christ. They treat their staff contemptibly. They are power hungry and manipulative. They may be harbouring secret adulterous affairs. They may be addicted to pornography. They may be paedophiles. They may treat their spouse terribly. They may rule over their congregations with pride and arrogance.

Yes, there are plenty of people in the church who claim to follow Christ but don't: people who claim to be Christians but whose lives throughout the week are lived in perpetual and flagrant disobedience to the commands of Christ.

Jesus, quoting from the prophet Isaiah (Isa 29:13), lamented this kind of hypocrisy when he said:

> "These people honour me with their lips, but their hearts are far from me." (Matthew 15:8)

Is that you? If it is, then you need to do something about it. You need to fall on your knees and repent. You need to stop merely calling Jesus Lord and actually start *obeying* him.

Of course, you will still slip up and sin occasionally. Your obedience will never be perfect, hence your ongoing need for his grace. But there should be a dramatic change. People around you should be able to see the difference. The grace of God is meant to transform us, from the inside out.

Did you notice the last line in the prayer that I asked you to pray at the end of the previous chapter? It said:

> *"I open my heart to you and ask that you will come into my life. Please fill me with Your presence and <u>strengthen me to follow you all the days of my life</u>."*

It's that 'follow' bit that is missing in some believers' lives. Has it been missing in yours? If so, then make a decision, right now, to begin to follow Christ as your Lord. Make a fresh pledge to turn from your sins, to truly turn your back on them, to let them go, to leave them behind, and begin to follow and obey Christ Jesus as your Lord and Saviour.

If that is your heart's desire, then here is a prayer you might like to pray:

> *"Lord Jesus, I confess that I have followed you in word only. My lips have confessed your name, but my life has denied your Lordship. I have not followed you as I should. I have lived in disobedience to your commands. In particular, I have ....*
>
> *Please forgive me. I kneel before you now, and pledge to follow you as my Lord. Please strengthen me to turn from sin and walk in newness of life. Please transform me from the inside out, by the power of your Holy Spirit, so that my life will glorify you from this day forward. I thank you for your grace, given so freely but at such a terrible cost to you. Thank you that through your death on the cross and your resurrection from the dead, I can be forgiven. Please*

help me to now live a life that honours you and reflects your grace to everyone around me. Amen."

∽

PERSONAL REFLECTION

The parable of the unforgiving servant is a very confronting parable. Significantly, Jesus told this parable, not to the Pharisees or to the general crowds, but to his select group of disciples: to those who were already on his team. So, it is right that we apply it to ourselves as Christians. This parable demands that we examine ourselves to assess whether we have truly been transformed by the grace of God. Once again, let me stress that God does not require perfection. Neither are we saved by our good works. But Jesus declared that a transformed, repentant life <u>must</u> follow our reception of God's grace, as the sign that we have truly come to know him. Spend some time reflecting on your life, in the following areas:

A TRANSFORMED INTER-PERSONAL LIFE. Has the grace of Jesus permeated your closest personal relationships? Do you consistently reflect his love and grace in the way you relate to those closest to you? Take a moment to think about the way you treat each person in your "inner circle". Do these people see you as a person who reflects the grace of Jesus? Can you identify specific actions or attitudes that you know God is wanting you to change or improve?

- The way you treat your spouse

- The way you treat your children

- The way you treat your parents and parents-in-law

- The way you treat your siblings

- The way you treat people in the church

A TRANSFORMED PRIVATE LIFE. Who are you when no one else is looking? Are there any habits that are not worthy of a follower of Christ? Are there actions or attitudes that you engage in which you would never consider doing if Jesus was physically at your side or if other church members could see you? Are there secret sins that you know God is wanting you to turn from? You know what to do! Make a fresh commitment, right now, to turn and walk away from those things. Ask God for his help and strength right now.

A TRANSFORMED CHURCH/WORK LIFE. As you serve God in your local church and in your workplace, do others see you as a person who reflects the love and grace of Christ in everything you do? Do they see Jesus in you? Or are you short-tempered? Easily upset? Controlling? Manipulative? Proud? Pushy? Demeaning? Unforgiving? Insensitive? What is your biggest area of weakness in this area? Ask for God's help that you might begin to serve him as a person of grace.

GROUP DISCUSSION QUESTIONS

1. Share your thoughts and impressions from this chapter. What was new to you? What was helpful? Is there anything you are still unsure about?

Read Acts 3:17-23

2. This is Peter's sermon to the crowd after healing a man who could not walk. What does Peter implore people to do, in verse 19? Notice that this involves both a turning 'from' and a turning 'to' something. Explain what this means.

3. In the same verse (v.3), we are told of two things that will result when we repent. What are they? Explain the second.

Read Psalm 51

4. Repentance has three aspects to it. The first is simply admitting and confessing our sins to God. This is exemplified in verses 3-5. Read through these verses again and discuss the various characteristics of David's confession. What kinds of things is he acknowledging?

5. The second aspect of repentance is asking for forgiveness. Read verses 1, 2, 7 and 9. What kinds of things characterise David's plea for forgiveness?

6. The third aspect of repentance is a commitment to change – to turn from habitual, defiant sin and lead a new life that seeks to honour God. Read verses 10-17. Examine this passage, verse by verse, and discuss the characteristics of David's pledge to live a changed life.

Read Galatians 5:16-26

This entire passage epitomises the repentant life; an ongoing commitment to turn from sin and be transformed by the inner working of God's Spirit. Throughout this passage there is a continual contrast being made between the 'flesh' and the 'spirit'.

7. Verses 17-18 describe a battle that is going on inside each of us every day. What is that battle? Explain it in your own words. Can you give practical, 'every-day' examples of this battle?

8. Compare verses 16, 18 and 25. They describe the Christian's ideal relationship with the Holy Spirit, using three similar terms. What are those three terms and what do they mean in practice?

9. Verses 19-21 define the kinds of sinful activity that God commands us to turn from if we are to be in relationship with him. What is the dire warning given in verse 21?

10. In verse 21, note the phrase, "those who live like this". The Bible is therefore not referring to a single "slip up", but something more endemic and ingrained. Explain this in your own words.

11. Examine the list of sins in verses 19-20. Which of these can sometimes become 'endemic' in the life of an individual Christian or in the life of a whole church culture?

12. Read verses 22-25. These are the qualities that ought to be apparent in the life of someone who is genuinely transformed by God's Holy Spirit. Notice the key word, 'fruit' in verse 22. What does this word imply" Why are these qualities described as "fruit"?

13. Read verse 24. What does it mean to "crucify the flesh with its passion and desires"?

5

SERVE JESUS THE KING

To this point, we have examined the twin concepts of faith and repentance as the two essential means of entering into, and maintaining, a saving relationship with Jesus. The twin responses of faith and repentance are the defining characteristics of the Christian life. The Christian lives each day trusting in Jesus for their forgiveness and seeking to honour Jesus in the way they live.

In this chapter we will examine a third key characteristic of the Christian life: service. Serving God does not save you, but it flows out of your saving relationship with Jesus. The Christian life is not merely one of merely sitting around waiting to go to heaven. When God reaches down and saves us, he gives us a place on his team and calls us to take part in the work of his Kingdom. The Christian is like a drowning man or woman who is plucked from a river, given a life jacket and then asked to jump back into the river to help save others. We are not meant to sit idly on the riverbank, comfortably rejoicing in our salvation while others continue to drown.

Serving the King – joining his great rescue mission – is not an optional extra. It is an essential part of being one of God's people. It is one of the three defining characteristics of the Christian life: faith, repentance and service. Faith and repentance are the *means* of initially receiving God's grace, whereas all three – faith, repentance and service – are the essential elements in our ongoing *response* to grace. These three defining characteristics of the Christian life are explicitly stated throughout the Bible, even from the earliest parts of the Old Testament:

> "Faithfully obey the commands I am giving you today [repentance and obedience], love the Lord your God [faith] and serve him with all your heart and soul [service]" (Deuteronomy 11:13).

Significantly, when Jesus spoke about the Christian life, he often defined it as a life of service:

> "No one can serve two masters. Either you will hate the one and love the other, or you will be devoted to the one and despise the other. You cannot serve both God and money." (Matthew 6:24)

> "Whoever serves me must follow me; and where I am, my servant also will be. My Father will honour the one who serves me." (John 12:26)

When we turn to Jesus in faith and repentance, we become his servant and he becomes our master. From that point on, we are called to serve him – to engage in the work of his kingdom on Earth. But what exactly does service entail? What kinds of things are we called to do?

Serving Jesus entails two distinct elements: reflecting his character and engaging in his mission.

REFLECTING THE CHARACTER OF JESUS

Jesus' whole life was characterised by kindness and compassion. He lived to demonstrate the love and kindness of God in practical ways. He healed the sick, he fed hungry crowds, he provided wine for an embarrassed wedding host, he restored dead children to their grieving parents. In all these ways and many more, Jesus demonstrated his compassion for people and his desire to extend God's love to them in practical ways. Many of Jesus' miracles were preceded by statements indicating that compassion was a key motive. For example, before he miraculously fed the four thousand, he stated:

> "I have compassion for these people; they have already been with me three days and have nothing to eat. I do not want to send them away hungry, or they may collapse on the way." (Matthew 15:32).

Before raising the widow's daughter back to life, we read:

> "When the Lord saw her, he felt compassion for her and said to her, 'Do not weep'." (Luke 7:13)

Indeed, the compassion of Jesus is evident in everything that Jesus did:

> "When Jesus landed and saw a large crowd, he had compassion on them and healed their sick." (Matthew 14:14)

> "Moved with compassion, Jesus touched their eyes; and immediately they regained their sight and followed Him." (Matthew 20:34)

For followers of Jesus today, serving Jesus means continuing to be his hands of love and compassion to a world of hurting, needy people. If this is how God lived when he came to Earth in the flesh, it is also how his servants must continue to live today. Indeed, Christians are specifically called to emulate Jesus – to live as he did. Jesus specifically stated this on two occasions:

> "Every disciple, after he has been fully trained, will be like his Teacher." (Luke 6:40)

> "The disciple is not above his teacher, nor a servant above his master. It is required for disciples to be like their teachers." (Matthew 10:24-25)

Jesus calls his people to continue to demonstrate his love and compassion in practical ways. This is why the Christian Church has, historically, been at the forefront of social welfare and charity. The first public hospitals were founded and funded by churches. The first public schools were founded and funded by churches. And still today, the majority of charities are run by Christian organisations. Sociological research also reveals that Christians are much more likely to give money to charity and to do volunteer work than people without religious convictions. Many individual churches also run programs for distributing meals to the needy and helping the homeless. In these and many other ways, God's people are continuing to serve God in demonstrating the compassion of Jesus. And God calls each of us to participate in this important work.

But, as important as all this is, this is not the church's mission. Churches who make this kind of social welfare and practical assistance the focus of their mission have completely missed the point.

ENGAGING IN THE MISSION OF JESUS

Acts of kindness and compassion were not Jesus' mission; nor should they be ours. Jesus did not come into the world merely to institute a program of social welfare for the sick and needy. His acts of kindness and compassion were reflections of his character; his 'modus operandi'. They were how he conducted himself as he went about his mission, but they were not his mission. Jesus tells us what his mission was:

> "The Son of Man came to seek and save the lost." (Luke 19:10)

Paul is equally clear in defining Jesus' mission:

> "Christ Jesus came into the world to save sinners." (1 Timothy 1:15)

This was Jesus' mission: to reach out to lost mankind, reconciling us to God by his atoning sacrifice for sin. Jesus had a much more important mission than merely making our lives on Earth a little more comfortable by healing some sicknesses and contributing some wine to a wedding. He was sent to rescue mankind who were facing an eternity of separation from God because of our rebellion. He came to fix a much bigger problem than the temporary inconveniences of sickness and poverty.

The healing of the paralysed man, in Mark 2:1-12, illustrates this, and the incident is worth quoting in full:

> "A few days later, when Jesus again entered Capernaum, the people heard that he had come home. ² They gathered in such large numbers that there was no room left, not even outside the door, and he preached the word to them. ³ Some men came, bringing to him a paralysed man, carried by four of them. ⁴ Since they could not get him to Jesus because of the crowd, they made an opening in the roof above Jesus by digging through it and then lowered the mat the

> man was lying on. ⁵ When Jesus saw their faith, he said to the paralysed man, "Son, your sins are forgiven." ⁶ Now some teachers of the law were sitting there, thinking to themselves, ⁷ "Why does this fellow talk like that? He's blaspheming! Who can forgive sins but God alone?" ⁸ Immediately Jesus knew in his spirit that this was what they were thinking in their hearts, and he said to them, "Why are you thinking these things? ⁹ Which is easier: to say to this paralysed man, 'Your sins are forgiven,' or to say, 'Get up, take your mat and walk'? ¹⁰ But so that you may know that the Son of Man has authority on earth to forgive sins," he said to the man, ¹¹ "I tell you, get up, take your mat and go home." ¹² He got up, took his mat and walked out in full view of them all. This amazed everyone and they praised God, saying, "We have never seen anything like this!" (Mark 2:1-12)

It is a fascinating story, isn't it? What is most relevant to our discussion is the priority that Jesus gives to the paralysed man's two problems. When Jesus looked at the man as he lay at his feet, he saw that he had two problems: a huge problem and a little problem. The little problem was that he was paralysed. It was only a little problem, because it would only last another 10 years or so, until he died. (Paraplegics and quadriplegics had a very short life expectancy in the first century). The man's paralysis was only temporary. Once he was dead, there would be no more paralysis.

But when Jesus looked at the man, he also saw that he had a far bigger problem. He saw that this paralysed man, just like every other human being, had rebelled against the living God. He had broken God's commands, not just once or twice, but many, many times. As a consequence, he was out of fellowship with God, and if he died in that state, he would be cut off from God forever! This is an ETERNAL problem, not just a temporary one.

And so Jesus decided to fix the eternal problem, the big problem, first. So he forgave the man's sin. This, in fact, is the whole reason Jesus came to Earth; to atone for sin and restore sinful humanity to God. This was his mission; a mission that would eventually take him to the cross, where he would die a cruel death to atone for the sins of the world.

The response of the religious leaders to Jesus' pronouncement of forgiveness to this man was outrage. They correctly understood that Jesus was claiming to be God, and they believed him to be committing blasphemy. But did you notice the fascinating question that Jesus then posed to them? He asked:

> *"Which is easier: to say to this paralysed man, 'Your sins are forgiven,' or to say, 'Get up, take your mat and walk'?" (verse 9).*

It is actually a really good question. What was easier for Jesus to say?

The words of physical healing that Jesus was about to say when he finally did heal the man's physical problem were very easy for him to say, because they only cost Jesus only a few words and a few moments of his power. But the words of forgiveness that Jesus spoke to this man, actually cost Jesus his life. Because in order to forgive that man, and every other person who will ever come to him in faith and repentance, Jesus had to go to the cross to die for our sins. It cost Jesus everything to say these words. But this was his mission. This was why he came to Earth. Jesus gave this man the most expensive gift, the most costly gift, the most important gift, first.

We need to take an important lesson from this incident. Our first and most important task is to share the message of salvation with the world. It is our mission, just as it was Jesus' mission. The practical acts of kindness and compassion that we also do in Jesus' name are meant to be signs that *confirm* our message and which commend the goodness of God to people. But they are never to be the focus of our mission itself. Did you notice that when Jesus finally healed the paralysed man, he indicated that this act of kindness was simply to *confirm* the more important act of forgiveness that he had just done:

> "But so that you may know that the Son of Man has authority on Earth to forgive sins, get up, take your mat and go home" (verses 10-11).

This story demonstrates the perfect synchronicity between acts of compassion and evangelism. By doing acts of compassion we reflect the *character* of Jesus, and by engaging in evangelism we are carrying out the *mission* of Jesus. The acts of compassion confirm and complement our message, but they are not the message itself. As Christians, we are *called* to reflect the character of Jesus and *commissioned* to proclaim the gospel. The two go hand in hand, but we must never confuse our *calling* with our *commission*. We must not so emphasise our acts of kindness and compassion that we neglect our mission.

Our commission to engage in God's great mission is most clearly described in the final exhortation by Jesus to his followers, known as 'The Great Commission'. Immediately before he ascended into Heaven, Jesus gathered his disciples together on a mountain in Galilee and gave them these final instructions:

> "All authority in heaven and on earth has been given to me. Therefore go and make disciples of all nations, baptising them in the name of the Father and of the Son and of the Holy Spirit, and teaching them to obey everything I have commanded you. And surely, I am with you always, to the very end of the age." (Matthew 28:18-20)

These were the last words Jesus spoke to his followers before he left the Earth and, as such, they carry enormous significance. Jesus was effectively giving the church its marching orders. He was defining our mission and passing the baton to us. He was effectively saying, *"I've done my part. Now you must carry on with my mission."*

God's primary concern is to save people from condemnation and bring them into his eternal kingdom. We must never forget this. We must not get confused into giving all our attention toward making people more comfortable here on Earth. Acts of compassion won't save people; they won't fix their biggest problem. As Christians, and as God's church on earth, everything we say and do, even our acts of compassion, must ultimately point people to Jesus as their Saviour and Lord – the One toward whom they must now turn in faith and repentance in order to be saved. This is the mission of the church, and it is the mission that God calls EVERY Christian to be part of.

The parable of the vineyard workers, in Matthew 20:1-16, graphically illustrates the essential nature of this mission for every Christian.

> *"For the kingdom of heaven is like a landowner who went out early in the morning to hire workers for his vineyard. ² He agreed to pay them a denarius[a] for the day and sent them into his vineyard. ³ "About nine in the morning he went out and saw others standing in the marketplace doing nothing. ⁴ He told them, 'You also go and work in my vineyard, and I will pay you whatever is right.' ⁵ So they went. "He went out again about noon and about three in the afternoon and did the same thing. ⁶ About five in the afternoon he went out and found still others standing around. He asked them, 'Why have you been standing here all day long doing nothing?' ⁷ "'Because no one has hired us,' they answered." He said to them, 'You also go and work in my vineyard.' ⁸ "When evening came, the*

> owner of the vineyard said to his foreman, 'Call the workers and pay them their wages, beginning with the last ones hired and going on to the first.' [9] "The workers who were hired about five in the afternoon came and each received a denarius. [10] So when those came who were hired first, they expected to receive more. But each one of them also received a denarius. [11] When they received it, they began to grumble against the landowner. [12] 'These who were hired last worked only one hour,' they said, 'and you have made them equal to us who have borne the burden of the work and the heat of the day.' [13] "But he answered one of them, 'I am not being unfair to you, friend. Didn't you agree to work for a denarius? [14] Take your pay and go. I want to give the one who was hired last the same as I gave you. [15] Don't I have the right to do what I want with my own money? Or are you envious because I am generous?' [16] "So the last will be first, and the first will be last."

At its simplest level, this parable is about GRACE. It is about God saving people from the spiritual unemployment line and giving them what they need rather than what they deserve. It is about unmerited forgiveness and being given a place in God's kingdom.

But did you notice what those who are saved, ('employed'), are expected to do? They are told to go and work in the owner's vineyard and join in the work of harvesting. EVERYONE who is saved is told to join in the work. Not just a few. Not just those who are particularly gifted. Everyone. In the parable, there are no people sitting on the sidelines, sipping chardonnay while they watch the others working in the vineyard. There are no idle spectators. Being rescued by God and given a place in his kingdom **necessarily** means joining in the **work** of his kingdom. God does not envisage someone joining his team but refusing to join in the work. That is not an option.

The vineyard in the parable represents the world, and the work that is taking place in the vineyard represents the work of evangelism: sowing the seeds of the gospel and harvesting souls for God's kingdom. And we are all called to be part of that: each and every one of us who have been saved by the grace of Jesus.

This book is called "*Reconnecting with God*", and the big point of this chapters is that when we connect with God, we must also connect with his mission. It's not an optional extra. We can't join God's team but refuse to work in his vineyard. Put simply, if you're not working in God's vineyard, you're not really on God's team.

But lest you become overwhelmed and daunted by this seemingly heavy expectation, let me unpack what it means. You are not necessarily called to preach on street corners and go door to door. Some people may feel called to do this, but I suspect that many Christians would rather beat themselves over the head with a lump of wood than engage in this kind of activity. God doesn't call everyone to be Billy Grahams or Martin Luthers. Some Christians are gifted evangelists, but most are not. And that is OK. God doesn't expect you to be someone you are not. He simply calls you to let your faith be obvious in the things you say and do.

Let me say that again. God calls you to let your faith be obvious in the things you say and do. He calls us to not be 'undercover Christians'. In the words of Jesus, in Matthew 5:16, he calls us to "*let our light shine*". In fact, it is worth quoting verses 15 and 16 in full:

> "*People do not light a lamp and put it under a basket. Instead, they set it on a stand, and it gives light to everyone in the house. In the same way, let your light shine before men, that they may see your good deeds and glorify your Father in heaven.*" (Matthew 5:15-16)

Do you see what Jesus is asking of us? He is asking us not to hide our light. He is asking us to stop being timid, undercover Christians, who are afraid to even mention our faith in Him. He is asking us to be courageous enough to place our light on a stand for all to see.

This means being willing to express our faith when an opportunity arises, perhaps in conversation with someone at work or at a social event, or even in a passing conversation with a stranger. This doesn't mean insensitively shoving the gospel down people's throats at every conceivable opportunity. It simply means courageously, yet sensitively and appropriately, responding when an obvious opportunity presents itself. And, in my experience, opportunities present themselves regularly. People who don't believe in God feel quite free to regularly express their views about life - about meaning and purpose, values and ethics. And when they do, I often take the opportunity to give my perspective as a Christian, thoughtfully and respectfully. Sometimes my comments are met with derision, but surprisingly, most of the time, people will respect me for my view, even if they disagree with it.

I encourage you to take the cover off your light. Let it shine. You may never lead a person to Christ, but you can be a link in the chain. The Christian who prays with someone as they give their life to Christ is the last link in the chain, but often there have been many other links in that person's journey towards faith: a series of other conversations and encounters that the person has had which have caused them to think about God and to question their own beliefs. We can all be a link in that chain. Just a simple comment, given prayerfully, respectfully and courageously, might resound in that person's mind long after they leave you. Let your light shine. And leave the cover in the bin where it belongs.

As well as being willing to speak of your faith in these kinds of passing encounters, you can also participate in God's mission in more proactive ways. You may be able to teach a Sunday School class, or help lead a youth group, or get involved with one of the many outreach ministries run by your own church. You could ask a friend to come along to a Bible study group. You could invite a friend to your church's men's breakfast, or ladies' craft morning or any of the other outreach events or special services that your church might hold from time to time.

At an even more basic level, you could join a community-based sporting or social group in order to cultivate genuine bonds of friendship with non-church people. You could invite your non-church friends for a meal, or have coffee with them at your favourite coffee shop. One of the great obstacles faced by the church in its outreach mission is the sad fact, confirmed by evidence-based research, that most Christians have very few meaningful friendships with non-church people. Why don't you make it your mission to cultivate genuine friendships with people outside the church and to pray for them, that they might one day come to faith? It might take many years before they are even willing to discuss matters of faith, let alone to step foot inside the church door or come to a church-run activity. But God needs his people to venture out of their Christian bubble and mix with people in the real world. We need to take the cover off our light.

CHALLENGE

Have you been on the sidelines of God's vineyard up to this point in your life? Have you been relatively disengaged with God's mission? It's never too late to join in. In the parable of the vineyard workers, the last workers were hired at 5pm, when all reasonable hope for 'employment' for the day was long gone. But God is a generous, gracious God. He is ever-searching for people to come and join him in his great rescue mission. Even at the very last hour, he will welcome you to his team and give you a place in his vineyard, to work alongside your brothers and sisters in the great task of leading others to the Saviour.

Decide today to connect more meaningfully, more intentionally, with God's great mission.

Come and join the team!

∼

PERSONAL REFLECTION

Is God's Spirit prompting you to become more engaged in God's great mission? Is there a sense in which you have been sitting on the sidelines? Before you get too overwhelmed or guilt-ridden, however, thinking that you must now add MORE things to your already overburdened schedule, the starting point is simply to begin to see the things you are ALREADY doing as opportunities to serve God. A fulltime mother with young children is already arguably one of the busiest people on the planet! Yet, she can see her role as a mother as a crucial act of service in nurturing her children, particularly as she seeks to lead them into a relationship with Jesus. Similarly, those with a job in the secular workforce can begin to see their relationships with their workmates as the harvest field that God has called them to work in.

Becoming more engaged in God's mission means, firstly, seeing the existing routines of your life as an opportunity to witness for Christ. How have you been going in doing this? Spend some time in prayer, asking for God's help to be a faithful 'vineyard worker' in the areas where God has already placed you.

Secondly, becoming more engaged in God's mission may also involve taking on an additional ministry. Your church has many ministries that are probably crying out for additional helpers and volunteers. Is there an area of service that you could volunteer for, that would suit your character and giftedness? Is God calling you to get more involved in the work of his kingdom and to sacrifice some of that time you spend watching TV or streaming services?

GROUP DISCUSSION QUESTIONS

1. Share your thoughts and impressions from this chapter. What was new to you? What was helpful? Is there anything you are still unsure about?

Read 1 Corinthians 15:58

2. The "Therefore" at the beginning of verse 58 refers back to the previous passage which has discussed the coming resurrection of the dead at the end of time and reminded us that we are only temporarily visiting this planet. How does this awareness shape Paul's exhortation to us in this verse?

3. What does it mean to *"always give yourselves fully to the work of the Lord"*? What will this look like in practical terms?

Read 2 Corinthians 5:14-15

4. Verse 15 describes the radical new paradigm (foundational philosophy of life) that should now characterise the Christian. What is it? What kinds of things might this mean, in practical terms?

5. If a person "no longer lives for themselves but for him who died for them and was raised again", how might this impact their priorities in terms of time, possessions and finances?

6. What is the primary motivation for this kind of selfless service? (see verse 14).

Read Matthew 25:14-30

This 'Parable of the Bags of Gold' is a powerful explanation of the importance that God places upon each of us living a life of service to him. The bags of gold represent our time and talents – the different abilities and characteristics that God endows each person with.

7. According to this parable, what is God's expectation of each of us?

8. What do the rewards in the parable represent? Are there different rewards in heaven? Get people in your group to look up and read out: Matthew 5:12, Matthew 16:27, 1 Corinthians 3:13-15, 2 Corinthians 5:10, Revelation 22:12.

9. Verses 26 to 30 describe God's displeasure and anger at those who 'bury their bags of gold'. What kind of attitude to life is this depicting?

10. Verse 30 is particularly harsh. What is this describing? What does this infer about the importance of serving God?

Read Ephesians 4:7-13

This is a key Bible passage that describes God's formula for creating a healthy church.

11. What do verses 7-8 teach us about the ability of each of us to contribute to the work of God's kingdom? (The word "grace" ['charis'] in verse 7 can, in this instance, also be translated "gifts").

12. Read verses 11-12. It is not the pastors and teachers of a church who are meant to do the "works of service". Who has God called to do this? What kinds of things might this involve?

13. According to verse 12, what is the role of the pastors and teachers?

14. Read verse 13. If the church operates like this, with everyone playing their part, what will be the result?

PART II
CONNECTING IN PRAYER

6

CONFRONT THE STRUGGLE OF PRAYER

If we are to connect with God at any depth, prayer is essential. You simply can't have a relationship with someone without talking to them! But praying to God regularly and consistently is not easy. It turns out that prayer is actually hard work.

Respected Christian theologian, John Stott, once stated, *"Prayer is my greatest struggle in the Christian life."* In James Houston's book, *The Transforming Power of Prayer*, he comments, *"Why write another book on prayer? The answer is simple - because a lack of prayer is so characteristic of today's church."* In his book, *Practical Religion*, J.C. Ryle writes, *"I have come to the conclusion that the great majority of professing Christians do not pray at all."*

Those are disturbing comments, aren't they? You may not be completely prayerless, but I think we can all agree that we struggle to pray consistently, regularly, at any great depth and for any significant length of time. Praying really is difficult! It's like pushing a rock uphill. If I asked a congregation of Christians to raise their hand if they don't pray as often and as deeply as they should, I suspect that every single hand would go up.

So, the first issue that needs to be addressed as we start this section on prayer is, *"Why is praying so difficult, and what can we do to address the problem?"*

I think it's very significant that Christians often speak of the need to be more *"disciplined"* in their prayer life. Because the point is, you only need to be disciplined about something that you don't absolutely love doing. You know you *should* do something, you know it's good for you, but you don't absolutely, passionately *love* it, so you have to *discipline* yourself to do it. On the other hand, if you really love doing something, if you are absolutely *passionate* about something, you don't have to be disciplined about doing it; you don't have to force yourself to do it, because you love it!

The difference between exercising and eating chocolate is a good example. Most people will say, *"I don't love exercise, but I know I should do it, because it's good for me, so I try to discipline myself to do it."* The discipline is needed in order to overcome our reluctance or lack of desire to do it. On the other hand, many people love eating chocolate. People who love chocolate, don't need to discipline themselves to eat it. You will never hear a person who loves chocolate say, *"I really should discipline myself to eat more chocolate."*

I am convinced that for most Christians, praying is more like exercise than eating chocolate. And when we speak about needing to be more *disciplined* in our prayer life, it really is an admission that our hearts aren't exactly exploding with a *desire* for prayer - a passionate *love* for prayer.

My hope is that these next three chapters might be a catalyst to ignite within you a passion for prayer; because if you get the passion, you won't really need the discipline.

An important starting point is to try to understand the root causes of our problem. Before we can find a solution, we need to understand the precipitating factors in our reluctance to pray. Why *don't* we have a passionate desire for prayer? Why is our desire for prayer weak, or spasmodic, or missing altogether?

WHY IS PRAYING SO DIFFICULT?

I want to suggest seven root causes of our problem:

1. PRAYER IS INTRINSICALLY HARD WORK

The Bible concedes that the nature of prayer is such that it is intrinsically difficult. We should not be surprised that it is hard work, for this is the experience of every Christian. Paul, in Colossians 4:12, writes:

> "Epaphras, who is one of you and a servant of Christ Jesus, sends greetings. He is always <u>struggling</u> in prayer for you ..."

The Greek word for "*struggle*" used here, "*agonizomai*" (ἀγωνίζομαι), means to fight or battle; to literally be in agony in one's struggle. It's a very confronting description of the battle of prayer. Intercessory prayer is hard work, and the word "struggle", used by Paul in this instance, is entirely appropriate to describe our ongoing experience of prayer. We struggle to stay focused. We struggle to know what to pray. We struggle to know the mind of God as we lift up the needs of our friends and family and church to the Lord. In prayer we wrestle and struggle to pray effectively, to frame our requests, to pray with fervour and faith, to remain focused and attentive.

This is our common experience of prayer, and there is a sense in which it always will be this way. Prayer is never going to be a walk in the park.

But I do think that prayer is much harder now for us than it has been for past generations, for several reasons. Which brings us to the second factor.

2. COMFORT AND COMPLACENCY

In Western society, most of us have everything we need. Compared to the vast majority of people on our planet, we live very affluent, comfortable lives. We have plenty to eat, nice homes fully of shiny gadgets, nice cars, access to health services and education, employment, entertainment ... and so on. Most of us in the Western world are richer, by far, than the majority of those living in developing countries or even those living in our own country in the past.

I have thousands of online contacts: Facebook friends, mailing list contacts and people who read my blog. Most of them are ministers, pastors or church leaders from around the world. I have noticed a significant difference in my correspondence with those living in underdeveloped countries, compared with those in developed countries. My Facebook friends from poorer countries are *always* talking about prayer and asking me to pray for them. I am bombarded with requests to pray for them; for their ministry, their family, their church, their town or village and their nation. They are constantly talking about their reliance on prayer and their need for others to pray with and for them. This is because their needs are often obvious and overwhelming - food, access to health services, poverty, hardship, disease, drought, famine, persecution, lack of facilities, lack of resources, etc. Those needs drive them to their knees. These dear Christian brothers and sisters are overwhelmingly conscious of their need for God's intervention on a daily basis.

On the other hand, my Facebook minister-friends in the developed world rarely talk about prayer and rarely ask me to pray for them. Because, in developed nations such as ours, we have everything we need (or so we think). We are comfortable. Our need for God is not nearly so obvious and our need for prayer is not nearly so desperate.

This is a big issue. Our comfort has made us complacent. It has sucked the urgency out of our prayer lives. It has diminished our sense of reliance upon God and dulled our passion for prayer. We are like the Laodiceans, in Revelation 3, to whom Jesus addressed these sobering words:

> *"To the angel of the church in Laodicea write: These are the words of the Amen, the faithful and true witness, the ruler of God's creation. I know your deeds, that you are neither cold nor hot. I wish you were either one or the other! So, because you are lukewarm—neither hot nor cold—I am about to spit you out of my mouth. You say, 'I am rich; I have acquired wealth and do not need a thing.' But you do not realise that you are wretched, pitiful, poor, blind and naked."* (Rev 3:14-17)

3. THE DECLINE OF PUBLIC PRAYER

The importance of prayer has also been de-emphasised in many modern church services. Many churches today are not practising and modelling public prayer as they did in the past. Numerous studies that have revealed that intercessory prayer in Christian gatherings has declined significantly in recent decades. Compared to 50 years ago, attendance at mid-week prayer meetings has also plummeted. Some studies have revealed that the average amount of time spent in corporate, intercessory prayer in church services today is a paltry one and a half minutes! That is because there are many modern churches that now have almost no intercessory prayer at all. In fact, in some churches, more time is devoted to the church announcements than to public prayer.

This has created a serious problem. If we aren't praying corporately - if we aren't modelling in our services the importance of prayer and demonstrating how to pray – it is little wonder that Christians aren't praying very much in their private lives.

4. COMMUNICATION & ENTERTAINMENT BOMBARDMENT

One of the greatest challenges to the personal spirituality of this generation is addiction to digital communication and entertainment. There is now a whole new exciting, digital world at our fingertips. We are constantly bombarded with messages, information, and entertainment. Our devices have a seductive allure that draws us in and captures our hearts and minds. At best, this can be a distraction and a time-waster. At worst, it can become an addiction that consumes us and captures our affection. I know many Christians, including church leaders and ministers, who are addicted to social media and who waste vast amounts of time scrolling through the latest posts or tweets.

Not only does the shiny digital world consume our time and make us less likely to engage in something as mundane and unappealing as prayer, it has also subtly altered people's ability to concentrate when they do pray. The constant stimulation of the digital world has significantly reduced the average person's attention span. People are now less able to spend a significant amount of time in something as mundane as prayer, without the visual and aural stimulation that they have become addicted to.

5. WESTERN PRAGMATISM

Compared to developing, third world nations, the Western world is dominated by pragmatism. This means that our first response to a problem or challenge is to fix it ourselves, rather than fall on our knees in prayer. When a problem or challenge arises, we form a committee, we strategise, we brainstorm, we re-vision, we set goals, we go to conferences, we read how-to books, we go to in-service training courses, we "Google" it. But in the developing world they often don't have all those resources and strategies. So, they just pray! It is their first and most natural response. And, to some extent, we in the developed world have lost that sense of prayer as our first and primary response.

6. WESTERN SCEPTICISM

Earlier last century, our society had at least an underlying belief in God and a basic acknowledgment of the supernatural realm. But the rise of secularism within society and the accompanying rapid decline in belief in God has resulted in a generalised scepticism in the Western world. Claims of miracles and answered prayer are regarded with extreme scepticism by society generally. They are explained away and dismissed. This is sadly exacerbated by documented cases of fraud and exaggeration by those claiming miraculous answers to prayer.

All of this has made us, as Westerners, more wary of believing in the miraculous. As a result, a degree of scepticism has seeped into the church, and we are less inclined to believe in and expect God's miraculous intervention in our world. Often our first response when we hear a testimony of a miraculous answer to prayer or some kind of healing is to wonder whether it has been exaggerated, or whether it was merely coincidental, or whether it can be explained by purely natural causes, or whether it is completely fake.

There is now, within the conservative church, a cautious, even suspicious scepticism that has weakened our faith in the miraculous. It has undermined our faith in the miracle-working power of God and this, in turn, has subtly diluted our confidence in the efficacy of prayer. And if we are no longer as confident in the miraculous *power* of prayer, then we are no longer as motivated to *engage* in prayer.

7. SPIRITUAL WARFARE

The Bible is very clear: there is a powerful evil spiritual force in the world that opposes God and the outworking of God's kingdom. The devil and his evil spiritual collaborators are hell-bent on opposing the work of God in our lives and in the world. And the last thing they want is for us to pray. Ephesians 6:12-18 states,

> *"For our struggle is not against flesh and blood, but against the rulers, against the authorities, against the powers of this dark world and against the spiritual forces of evil in the heavenly realms. ... With this in mind, be alert and always keep on praying for all the Lord's people."*

This passage is so important for our understanding of prayer. A large part of the reason why prayer is so difficult is that there are evil spiritual beings doing all they can to stop us from praying. Our struggle is *not* just against flesh and blood. When you find it difficult to pray, you are not just fighting your own laziness, your own lack of commitment, your own lack of faith - you are wrestling with the forces of evil *who do not want you to pray!*

I want you to note how Paul ends this explanation of Satan's opposition in Ephesians 6. He concludes by *urging* us to pray all the more. He says in verse 18, **"With this in mind"** - in other words, now that you know that an evil spiritual being is messing with your mind and messing with your heart; now that you know that it's not just your own slackness you are fighting against - *"With this in mind, BE ALERT"* - in other words WAKE UP - stop being a helpless victim - *"... be alert and always keep on praying for all the Lord's people."* In other words, now that you know you're in the middle of a battle, it should motivate you to pray all the more. In fact, you need to get a bit angry about this! Someone is messing with your mind! You need to dig in, grit your teeth and say, *"No way! I am not going to give in! I AM GOING TO PRAY! AND YOU ARE NOT GOING TO STOP ME!"*

THE EXAMPLE OF MOSES

Nowhere is the battle of prayer more graphically illustrated, and its efficacy more vividly portrayed, than in the story of Moses and the battle against the Amalekites, in Exodus 17:8-13.

> *"The Amalekites came and attacked the Israelites at Rephidim. Moses said to Joshua, "Choose some of our men and go out to fight the Amalekites. Tomorrow I will stand on top of the hill with the staff of God in my hands." So, Joshua fought the Amalekites as Moses had ordered, and Moses, Aaron and Hur went to the top of the hill. As long as Moses held up his hands, the Israelites were winning, but whenever he lowered his hands, the Amalekites were winning. When Moses' hands grew tired, they took a stone and put it under him and he sat on it. Aaron and Hur held his hands up—one on one side, one on the other—so that his hands remained steady till sunset. So, Joshua overcame the Amalekite army with the sword."*

In case you are not familiar with what was going on in that incident, the Amalekites were a particularly wicked group of people who, for centuries, had indulged in sorcery, witchcraft, human sacrifice and sexual immorality of all kinds. After centuries of them ignoring God's repeated warnings (for example, God's warnings to them in Exodus 17:16 and 1 Samuel 15:2-3), the Lord finally declared judgment on them. When the Amalekites decided to attack God's people, the Lord allowed the Israelites to defend themselves and, in so doing, they became the agents of God's long-awaited judgment on the Amalekites.

Of particular significance for our current discussion was the action of Moses. The raising of his arms on top of the hill represented his prayers to God. He was beseeching God to intervene and to grant the Israelites victory. As long as his arms were raised in supplication to God, the Israelites were winning. But as his arms grew tired and drooped, the Israelites began to lose, until Moses' assistants, Aaron and Hur, propped his arms up again, and the Israelites began to win once more.

It is an extraordinary story! A visually stunning depiction of the power of prayer! Although there were tens of thousands of people fighting in the valley below, it was the prayers of just one man on the hill that determined the final outcome of that battle. The prayers of one man determined the fate of the whole nation at that point!

That story is in the Bible for a reason. It is there as a lesson for us. And it is not just a *metaphor* for prayer - it is an ACTUAL historical example of the incredible, extraordinary power of prayer! It teaches us that prayer that is prompted by God's Spirit and prayed by those who are in right relationship with Him really can change the world!

Paul, in 1 Timothy 2:8, says:

"*I want people everywhere to pray, lifting up holy hands ...*"

This statement is a direct reference to this story in the Old Testament where Moses lifted his hands in prayerful supplication and changed the fate of a nation. Paul is pointing out the responsibility and calling that God has now given to ALL Christians; not just to Moses, not just to the minister or priest of the church. God calls us *all* to intercede on behalf of his kingdom, because our prayers really do change things!

Do you want to see revival break out in your community and in our nation? Then we must take hold of the weapon that God has given us. We must recognise that while prayer will always be a struggle - a battle - God calls us all to take our place in that battle for the sake of his Kingdom. We must pray! We must overcome the struggle with our own laziness. We must push through the fogginess of our minds. We must refuse to be sidetracked and distracted by the allure of the modern world. We must refuse to be deceived by its pragmatism and unbelief. And, above all, we must consciously and intentionally take our stand against the demonic forces that are seeking to stop us from praying. We must cease being victims in this 'prayer war' and start being the conquerors that God calls us all to be.

Charles Spurgeon once said:

> "Prayer pulls the rope below, and the great bell rings above in the ears of God. Some Christians scarcely stir the bell, for they pray so languidly; others give but an occasional tug at the rope; but the ones who truly connect with heaven are those who grasp the rope boldly and pull continuously, with all their might"

There is no greater appointment you have in your day and in your week than the appointment to come into the presence of God and pray; to pray on behalf of your friends and family, your church, your community, your nation and the outworking of God's Kingdom on Earth. That appointment has the potential to change the world! The battle is worth it.

∽

PERSONAL REFLECTION

Is God calling you to reinvigorate your prayer life? What are the major obstacles stopping you from praying more regularly? Is social media a distraction? Are there things that consume your time and attention and affection. Spend some time identifying them and asking God to help you overcome them.

Is your desire to pray weak or non-existent? Then you need to pray about that as a starting point.

Can you decide on a specific place and time where you can guarantee to get some 'alone time' to spend even just a few minutes each day in prayer? What about as you travel to work? Or after you drop children at school? Or early in the morning before anyone else in your household gets up. If you don't establish a definite routine, prayer will almost certainly not happen consistently.

GROUP DISCUSSION QUESTIONS

1. Share your thoughts and impressions from this chapter. What was new to you? What was helpful? Is there anything you are still unsure about?

Read Mark 1:35-39

2. The day before this event, Jesus had a very busy day of ministry, preaching in the Synagogue and then healing a huge crowd of sick people in Capernaum until late at night. In the light of this, how does verse 35 impress you? What does it say about the priority that Jesus placed upon prayer?

Read Luke 5:15-16

3. Verse 15 indicates the growing busyness of Jesus' ministry. In the light of this, what can we learn about the importance of prayer from verse 16?

Read Colossians 4:2

4. What does it mean to be "devoted" to prayer?

5. Why are we told to be "watchful" as we pray? What are we meant to be watching for?

Read Matthew 6:5-13

6. In this model prayer, taught by Jesus, identify all the key elements that make up a balanced prayer life and discuss each one:

Verse 9:

Verse 10:

Verse 11:

Verse 12:

Verse 13:

Read Ephesians 6:10-18

7. Notice Paul's statement in verse 18; *"With this in mind, be alert and always keep on praying"*. With what in mind?

8. How might an awareness of the spiritual battle that we are in the midst of help us become more determined to pray regularly?

9. Paul's exhortation in verse 18 to "pray in the Spirit" does not mean praying in tongues (at least not on this occasion). What do you think Paul means? How often does he exhort us to do

this?

Read Exodus 17:8-13

10. As well as being a description of an actual historical event, this is also a deeply metaphorical passage. What do these following elements represent?

The battle against the Amalekites:

Moses' raised arms:

Moses' helpers:

11. What are the major "battles" facing your church and your community at the moment? Perhaps you might find it helpful to actually note these down as prayer points and pray about them at the end of your study.

12. What are the major battles that members of your group are facing, personally? Write them down as well.

13. Spend some time praying for those issues now.

7

DARE TO PRAY IN FAITH

Mark 11:24 "Therefore I tell you, whatever you ask for in prayer, believe that you have already received it, and it will be yours."

When I was a young Christian, I went on a beach mission to Easts Beach, near Kiama. Towards the end of the week, we planned an outreach barbeque for adults – free sausage sandwiches for everyone in the camping area at 6:00pm. We were planning to mingle and chat with our fellow campers, and a brief gospel talk would be presented at some point during the evening. But on the day of the barbeque, it began raining and kept raining all day. The clouds set in and the forecast was for continual rain for the next two days. People from the campsite kept asking us all day if the barbeque would be cancelled, but we kept assuring them that it wouldn't. Our team gathered together that afternoon and prayed for a miracle – that God would stop the rain so that our barbeque could go ahead. As the time for the barbeque approached, the sky above us cleared. A circle of clear sky appeared directly overhead, while all around us in every direction the rain kept falling in a circular curtain! The barbeque went ahead and the gospel was preached, and after it was over, the circle of clear sky closed over us once more, and it started pouring!

That was a transformative event for me as a young Christian, because it showed me that prayer actually works!

I want you to be absolutely convinced that prayer works. I want you to be believe, with all your heart, the promise of Jesus in Mark 11:24:

> "Therefore, I tell you, whatever you ask for in prayer, believe that you have already received it, and it will be yours."

Jesus is asking us to pray with so much faith that we are completely confident that our prayers will be answered. It is an extraordinarily bold kind of faith that Jesus is asking of those who would approach God in prayer. It almost seems too presumptuous, doesn't it?

In order to pray that kind of faith-filled prayer, there are a number of things a person must believe first. Let me walk you through the essential elements of the prayer of faith:

1. THERE IS A GOD

If you don't believe this, you're just talking to yourself. Christian prayer is not a mindless mantra that merely makes us feel good. True prayer makes a connection with the living God. Hebrews 11:6 tells us,

> "Without faith it is impossible to please God, because anyone who comes to him must <u>believe that he exists</u>."

Self-confessed atheist, J.D. Moyer, in his article, "*Why, As An Atheist, I Pray*" speaks of enjoying the practice of prayer, even though he believes there is no God:

> "I enjoy praying because I feel like I am talking to someone more powerful than us, who loves us. Prayer can satisfy a sort of psychological craving, an inner void, even though the entity I'm addressing exists only in my mind — a construct, yet it feels like I'm addressing someone outside of myself — an externality".

But if that is all prayer is for you – just talking to an imaginary construct – then you really are just wasting your time. The starting point of meaningful prayer has got to be that you believe there is a personal God.

2. GOD CAN HEAR MY PRAYERS

This takes a little more faith; to believe that in the midst of all the millions of prayers that are being prayed at any one time on Earth, God can actually hear *you*. Yet the Bible assures us that this is so. The Psalmist says:

> "Before a word is on my tongue, you know it completely O Lord" (Psalm 139:4).

How's that for excellent hearing? You don't even need to speak the words aloud – all you need to do is pray something in the silence of your heart and mind, and God instantly hears you.

3. GOD CAN ANSWER MY PRAYERS

This is the belief that God is all-powerful and that nothing is impossible for him.

A mother was once praying with her son before he went to sleep. The little boy prayed, *"Dear God, please bless mummy and daddy, and grandma and grandpa. And please make Paris the capital city of England. Amen."* His mother said, *"That's a strange thing to pray. Why did you pray that?"* The little boy replied, *"Because that's what I wrote in my geography test today."*

I love the faith of little children! They have no trouble believing that God can do the impossible. You and I, as adults, know that while God can do the impossible, he is not going to do the illogical, but children have a simple trusting faith in God. That is why Jesus, on one occasion, spoke about our need to approach God with the faith of a little child; the faith that says *"Nothing is impossible for God"* (Luke 1:37), and the faith that believes that *"God is able to do immeasurably more than all we ask or imagine"* (Eph 3:20).

Do you believe that? How big is your concept of God? Because the God to whom we pray is the One who created untold billions of galaxies by simply speaking them into being. Take the time one night to go outside and look up at the stars and think to yourself, *"the God who made all that, can do immeasurably more than all I ask or imagine."* If you are having trouble praying in faith, lift your eyes to the heavens – literally! King David declared:

> *"The heavens declare the glory of God; the skies proclaim the work of his hands." (Psalm19:1)*

4. GOD WANTS TO ANSWER MY PRAYERS

I suspect it is at this point that many of us struggle in our prayer life. We find it difficult to believe that God is interested in our needs and inclined to answer our requests. After all, we are nobodies and God is very busy running the universe. *Surely, he is out there somewhere doing important stuff, and he really isn't going to bother with my little prayers. God may be interested in answering the prayers of the great saints, but I am a long way down the pecking order.*

Can you relate to those kinds of thoughts?

If you have ever had those kinds of doubts, you need to re-read the Gospels and take note of how often Jesus implores us to "ask" God for things in prayer. Again and again, when speaking to general crowds of people as well as to his disciples specifically, Jesus exhorts people to present their requests to God. He urges us to ask God for things. Implicit in these many exhortations is the assurance that God WANTS to hear and answer our requests. We are not bugging him when we pray. He welcomes us to petition him with our needs and the needs of others, because, in so doing, we acknowledge our dependence upon him and he is glorified. These many exhortations by Jesus carry with them an astonishingly clear declaration of God's desire to answer our prayers:

Matthew 7:7 "Ask, and it will be given to you; seek and you will find; knock and the door will be opened to you."

John 14:13-14 "I will do whatever you ask in my name, so that the Father may be glorified in the Son. You may ask me for anything in my name, and I will do it."

John 15:16 "The Father will give you whatever you ask in my name"

John 16:23 "I tell you the truth, my Father will give you whatever you ask for in my name"

John 16: 24 "Until now you have not asked for anything in my name. Ask and you will receive, and your joy will be complete."

Let me share a practical example from my own life, of an instance when God answered what I deemed to be a relatively insignificant prayer.

One weekend in 2001, my wife and I and our two kids were staying for a few days with my parents at Forster, Australia. Late one afternoon, my young daughter suddenly realised that her watch was missing. She remembered taking it off while we were at the beach earlier that day. She had placed it in her towel while she went for a swim but couldn't remember seeing it after that. We concluded that it must have fallen out onto the sand when she unwrapped the towel to dry herself. The watch had sentimental value and my daughter was very upset.

We immediately rushed back to the beach, which was only 5 minutes away. When we got there the sun was setting and the beach was completely deserted. The lifeguards had long since packed up and left, and there was literally no one on the beach. We stood looking around trying to gauge roughly where our towels had been, but it was impossible to tell without the lifeguard flags with which to orient ourselves. We ended up standing in the middle of a vast stretch of beach staring hopelessly at the sand around us. I remember saying to my wife, "It's hopeless. We'll never find it." My wife, however, refused to give in. "Let's pray and ask God to help us," she suggested.

I remember thinking, "I'm sure God has much more important issues to be dealing with than finding a teenage girl's watch!", but I didn't dare say it aloud. Not wanting to seem unspiritual, I agreed to lead our family in a brief prayer. We held hands and I simply asked God if he would help us find the watch. I must be totally honest with you at this point: I did not believe that God was going to answer that prayer. Even as I prayed, I was already starting to formulate in my mind a logical, reasonable explanation to give to my wife and children as we drove home empty-handed. I would explain to them that God doesn't always answer our prayers the way we would like. I would explain that God is much more concerned with transforming us and changing us on the inside than in helping us keep track of our possessions.

I was completely unprepared for what happened next.

As soon as I finished praying and we all said, "Amen", my wife knelt down in the sand, plunged her hand into a drift of sand and squealed. I thought she had been bitten by a crab! She hadn't. She drew her hand out of the sand and held up my daughter's watch! It had been buried under about 10cm (4 inches) of sand. It was literally the very first plunge of my wife's hand. In all that vast, empty beach, we had somehow come to stand precisely where our towels had been and, even more amazingly, my wife's hand had zeroed in on the watch like a radar-guided missile. To say that I was surprised would be a complete understatement.

Someone could claim that finding my daughter's watch in that way on the very first plunge of a hand was simply a fluke – a product of brute chance. But what kind of fantastically small probability are we talking about? We had absolutely no idea where our towels had been. For all we knew we could have been 50 or even 100 metres away from our previous spot on the beach.

I could multiply these stories a hundredfold – instances from my own life and the life of my family where we have seen God's miraculous hand at work. Only very occasionally have they been spectacular miracles. Mostly, in fact nearly always, they have been much more mundane things involving phone calls, emails, watches and even tinier details of everyday life that God mysteriously "tweaks" when we ask for guidance or help of some kind.

Nineteen times in the Gospels – yes, nineteen! - Jesus pleads with his followers to "ask" for things in prayer. God *wants* you to pray. He welcomes your prayers. God wants you to ask him for things, including for his guidance. Why? Because he loves you and it honours him when we submit our needs to him and acknowledge our dependence upon him.

5. GOD WILL ANSWER MY PRAYERS

But to pray in faith means more than merely believing that God WANTS to answer my prayers. It means believing that He WILL.

A Sunday school class was encouraged to write individual letters to send to a missionary they were supporting overseas. However, the Sunday School teacher told her class to keep their letters short and to not expect an answer. The teacher told them that missionaries were very busy people and that we shouldn't be surprised if they don't have time to answer our letters. Accordingly, a little girl in the class wrote the following letter: *"Dear Mr Smith. I am praying for you. I am not expecting an answer"*.

Without realising it, that little girl summed up the prayer life of many Christians. We often pray, but we don't really expect an answer. (Just like me with the lost watch on the beach). And when an answer does come, we're surprised! No wonder some Christians rarely see answered prayer! In fact, that is precisely what James says, in James 1:6-7.

> *"When you ask, you must believe and not doubt, because the one who doubts is like a wave of the sea, blown and tossed by the wind. Such a person should not expect to receive anything from the Lord"*

Jesus said much the same thing on several occasions:

> Matthew 9:29 *"According to your faith will it be done to you"*

> Matthew 21:22 *"If you believe, you will receive whatever you ask for in prayer"*

> Luke 17:6 *"If you have faith as small as a mustard seed, you can say to this mulberry tree, 'Be uprooted and planted in the sea,' and it will obey you.*
>
> Mark 11:24 *"Therefore I tell you, whatever you ask for in prayer, believe that you have already received it, and it will be yours."*

But before we all begin to pray for that Lamborghini or that million-dollar yacht, there's one important issue we need to clarify. Did you notice in the verses listed under the previous point, ('God Wants To Answer My Prayers'), that there is one little phrase that is common to them all? – *"in my name"*. When Jesus uses that term, he is defining a very important parameter for prayer, and it has two key elements to it:

A. Praying in Jesus' name means praying in a right relationship with Him. We approach the Father through our relationship with His Son:

> John 15:7 *"If you remain in me, and my words remain in you, ask whatever you wish, and it will be given to you."*

Christians are the only people on Earth whom God has *promised* to answer their prayers – because they are the only ones in relationship with His Son.

Occasionally, I've had people who are not yet Christians say to me, *"I've tried praying and it doesn't work"*. In this situation, I try to explain the contradiction that is involved when a non-Christian – someone who is currently refusing to accept the Lordship of Christ over their lives – asks God for some kind of help. Effectively, such a person is pushing Jesus away with one hand while simultaneously holding out the other hand to God and asking him for a favour. It is hardly surprising that, in most cases, God is not going to answer that kind of prayer – not until the person has prayed the most important prayer of all, the prayer that turns to Christ in faith and repentance and receives from him the forgiveness that he offers; the prayer that makes peace with God by coming into a relationship with his Son. Until a person has prayed that prayer, God is not going to take much notice of any other prayer.

Being in a right relationship with Jesus – "remaining" in him – infers the necessity of an ongoing commitment to following him as Lord. To "remain" in fellowship with Jesus, means a commitment obeying him. A person who may once have prayed to receive Christ as Lord and Saviour, but who is now living in flagrant disobedience to his commands in some area of their life, should not expect to have their prayers answered. Thus, the psalmist writes:

> "If I had cherished sin in my heart, the Lord would not have listened." (Psalm 66:18)

This does not infer that you must be perfect in my obedience to God's commands in order to have your prayers responded to, for if that was the case, no one would have their prayers answered! The key word in the above verse is 'cherished'. The psalmist is speaking of someone who is caught up in a repeated, deliberate sin, and is unrepentant. Such a person should not expect God to answer their prayers until they repent and recommit themselves to following Christ as their Lord.

B. Praying in Jesus' name also means praying in accordance with Jesus' character and will:

> 1 John 5:14 "This is the confidence we have in approaching God; that if we ask anything <u>according to his will</u>, he hears us. And if we know that he hears us – whatever we ask – we know that we have what we asked of him."

What sorts of things are definitely going to be in God's will? Well, I'm pretty sure a Lamborghini is not high on God's list of kingdom priorities for me! What Jesus is referring to is anything that extends God's kingdom on Earth and brings glory to his name. That includes a huge range of things, from praying for revival for our nation, right down to praying for our simple daily needs, just as Jesus taught us to pray. Consider the following prayer, for example:

> *"Lord, please help me to find the money to pay this bill. Please give me strength for today and help me to make it to the end of the day without throttling the kids!"*

This is a good prayer to pray, and it is spiritual – because you are expressing your dependence on God and your need for his help. And Jesus promises that if you pray this prayer as a faithful, repentant, humble Christian, God will answer you.

If we are in a right relationship with Jesus, if we are convinced that what we are praying for is in accordance with God's character and will, and if we are praying selflessly and humbly, without obvious unconfessed sin standing between us and God, then Jesus urges us to pray in *faith*. He urges us to pray with extraordinary boldness and confidence - not confidence in ourselves or in the efficacy of our prayers, but confidence in the greatness and generosity of Almighty God.

Do you want to see a revival in your church? In your town? In your community? In your own life, perhaps? To see your friends and loved ones turn to Christ in faith and repentance? Then, God is calling you to pray. To pray in faith. To dare to pray boldly and confidently, believing in him for a miracle.

A FINAL INSPIRING STORY

The evacuation of the Allied army from Dunkirk in May 1940 is the story of a miraculous answer to prayer. On May 10th, 1940, Hitler unleashed a military onslaught on France and Belgium. Within days the British Army, along with many allied soldiers, found themselves with their backs to the sea and hemmed in by enemies. They were vastly outnumbered and underprepared, and were facing complete annihilation. The situation was so dire that Winston Churchill prepared a press statement advising the public of an unprecedented military catastrophe involving the capture or death of over a third of a million soldiers - almost the entire British army.

But it didn't happen. On May 23rd, King George VI requested that the following Sunday should be observed as a National Day of Prayer. On that Sunday, the entire nation devoted itself to prayer in an unprecedented way. Eyewitnesses and historical photographs confirm overflowing congregations in places of worship across the land. Long queues formed outside cathedrals and churches. The whole of Great Britain came to a standstill and gathered together to pray. That same day, an urgent request went out for boats of all sizes and shapes to cross the English Channel to rescue the besieged army, a call ultimately answered by around 800 private vessels.

As a result of that day of prayer, a number of miraculous events unfolded:

Firstly, in a decision that infuriated the German generals and still baffles historians, Hitler ordered his army to come to a halt. Had they pressed on and continued to fight, the complete destruction of the British forces would have been inevitable, and the war would have taken a different, darker, more terrible path. Yet, for three days the German tanks and soldiers stood idle while the allied evacuation unfolded.

Secondly, God miraculously tweaked the weather. Terrible weather on the Monday and Tuesday grounded the German Luftwaffe, allowing Allied soldiers to march unhindered to the beaches.

Thirdly, on the following day, Wednesday, the scheduled day of the mass evacuation, the sea was extraordinarily calm, despite the storm that had grounded the Luftwaffe during the previous two days. This allowed the hundreds of tiny private English yachts and other vessels to sail right into the shore to load the evacuees. Photographs show lines of soldiers walking across planks between small skiffs and row boats and stepping directly onto yachts and other small craft which were anchored in the miraculously calm shallow water along the shore.

By the time the German Army was finally ordered to renew its attack, over 338,000 troops had been snatched from the beaches; a third of a million! Many of them were to return four years later to liberate Europe.

Some people might say these extraordinary events were all merely a fortunate coincidence, but I think not. It certainly wasn't considered a coincidence at the time. Three weeks later, Sunday, June 9th was declared a National Day of Thanksgiving, and the entire nation went to church again to thank God for his deliverance. Winston Churchill subsequently referred to the evacuation as 'the miracle of Dunkirk'.

An entire nation prayed, and God answered!

For some reason that I'll never fully understand, God has decided that our prayers play a crucial role in the outworking of events on earth. And that is why Jesus repeatedly implored his disciples to ask and ask again, and keep on asking for things in His name, because our prayers really do make a difference!

PERSONAL REFLECTION

Spend some time reflecting on your own prayers. Do you pray with this kind of faith and confidence?

What are some faith blockers that may hinder your prayer life?

Do you tend to pray "safe" prayers – prayers that are general and non-specific?

Make a list of specific things that God may be challenging you to begin praying about. Perhaps the conversion of some specific people. Or perhaps issues in your own life that require God's help and strength to overcome.

Spend some time, now, praying in faith for God's miraculous intervention in those situations. Approach the throne of grace with confidence!

GROUP DISCUSSION QUESTIONS

1. Share your thoughts and impressions from this chapter. What was new to you? What was helpful? Is there anything you are still unsure about?

Read Mark 11:22-25

2. Notice in verse 22 that we are not called to have faith in the power of prayer. What is the basis of our faith and confidence when we approach God in prayer? Be specific. What is it about God that we are exercising faith in?

3. Verse 24 contains a strong promise, but it is grounded in a strong condition. What kind of faith is being requested of us as we pray?

4. Why, in the midst of a discussion about prayer, does verse 25 seem to divert to an exhortation to forgive others. What is the relevance?

Read Hebrews 4:14-16

5. According to this passage, what is the basis for our confidence that God will hear and answer our prayers?

Read and compare Matthew 9:28-29 and Matthew 13:58

6. Why do you think God requires faith in order to answer our prayers and grant our requests?

7. The question that Jesus asked the blind man in Matthew 9:28 is extremely important: "Do you believe that I am able to do this?" Do you think there are times when we pray for something because we know we should, but in our hearts we may actually doubt that God will ever do it? Give practical examples.

Read James 1:5-8

8. This is another description of the direct, inextricable link between faith and answered prayer. Notice the imperative, *"you MUST believe and not doubt"* in verse 6. What clear warning does this passage give regarding prayers that are full of doubt? (see verse 7).

9. Why does James describe such a person as "double minded?"

Read 1 John 5:13-15

10. Who are the only people that can have confidence that God will hear and answer their prayer?

11. What does it mean to pray "according to his will"? How can we know what God's will is?

12. Spend some time making a list of prayer points now: needs in your own lives, in the lives of others, in the life of your church and in the nation and the world generally.

13. Pray for those things now. In particular, if you can see that the meeting of those needs would bring glory to God and would extend his kingdom on Earth, you can be sure that these are things that would be "according to his will". Therefore, pray for them with great boldness and faith! Remember, Jesus never criticised anyone for having too much faith!

8

PRAY WITH PERSISTENCE

The Bible urges us to pray with persistence. This means not just praying for something once and then leaving it in God's hands, but praying for the same thing over and over, again and again, day by day, until the answer comes. But does this seem counter-intuitive to you? Surely, if we pray in faith, just one heartfelt, passionate prayer ought to be enough.

But that is not the case. The Bible is very clear about this: God requires persistence from us in our prayers as a sign of our faith and our complete dependence upon him. This is evident in the parable of the persistent widow that Jesus told, in Luke 18:

> "Then Jesus told his disciples a parable to show them that they should always pray and not give up. 2 He said: "In a certain town there was a judge who neither feared God nor cared what people thought. 3 And there was a widow in that town who kept coming to him with the plea, 'Grant me justice against my adversary. 4 For some time he refused. But finally, he said to himself, 'Even though I don't fear God or care about people, 5 yet because this widow keeps bothering me, I will see that she gets justice, so that she doesn't

wear me out!' 6 And the Lord said, "Listen to what the unjust judge says. 7 And will not God bring about justice for his chosen ones, who cry out to him day and night? Will he keep putting them off? 8 I tell you, he will see that they get justice, and quickly. However, when the Son of Man comes, will he find faith on the earth?" (Luke 18:1-8)

The underlying message of this parable is really quite simple. If an unjust judge, who does not fear God and does not care about people can eventually be swayed to grant a person's request through sheer dogged persistence, how much more will God, who DOES love us, be inclined to grant our requests when we persist in prayer.

The first line of that Bible passage is key:

> "Jesus told his disciples a parable to show them that they should always pray and <u>not give up</u>."

I think we often pray and then give up. We pray for something once or twice, but when the answer doesn't immediately arrive, we stop praying. We promise to pray for someone, then we either forget to pray at all, or we pray just a few times and then give up.

It is not just our slackness that is causing this lack of persistence. I suspect that, for many of us, we feel that by continually coming to God with the same request over and over again, we are badgering him. Perhaps we think that God will get annoyed, or that constantly asking for the same thing again and again is an indication of a *lack* of faith. But this is not the case at all.

The persistent widow in the parable who did, indeed, badger the judge continually is presented by Jesus as a model for us to follow. Jesus effectively commends her to us and tells us that we should be like her in our prayers! We should *"always pray and not give up"* (v.1). We should *"cry out to God day and night"* (v.7). Jesus is telling us very clearly that God is looking for people who will approach him in prayer just like that widow; people who will pray tenaciously and doggedly, crying out to him day and night until the answer is given.

Of course, there are some occasions when God, in his sovereignty, chooses to answer a prayer almost immediately. There have been more than a few of these instances in my own life. But in many cases, perhaps most, the answers are much slower in coming, requiring us to persist in our prayers for many months or even years.

Just why God chooses to answer some prayers immediately while others are not answered for many years is not clearly explained in the scriptures. There is a mystery about prayer that remains obscure to us. The complex interplay between the supernatural realm and our physical world is a mystery that we can only dimly perceive. There is much we don't understand about the relationship between our feeble prayers and the sovereign will of Almighty God. The Bible does not give us a detailed explanation of how it all works. We are simply exhorted to continue praying until the answer arrives.

Furthermore, the Bible seems to urge us to exhibit a surprising degree of urgent insistence in our prayers. Far from approaching the throne of grace with grovelling timidity, this parable and other New Testament passages that have a bearing on our theology of prayer urge us to pray with a boldness and dogged determination that is almost shocking. The persistent widow did not come meekly into the judge's presence, apologising for intruding and asking, *"If it's not too much trouble, would you mind helping me?"* No. She stood outside his house, stubbornly crying out to him *"day and night"*, annoying him and refusing to back down until she got her request! This was not polite petitioning.

Of course, we need to be careful that we don't infer too much from this. Jesus is not indicating that we can be rude and demanding toward God in our prayers. He is simply commending this woman's bold persistence and boldness, and is encouraging us to be like her in our prayers.

Jesus' admiration for this kind of stubborn persistence is seen in an encounter he had with a Canaanite woman, recorded for us in Matthew 15:21-28. The woman approached Jesus with a request for him to heal her daughter, but Jesus initially refused, saying that he was sent to minister to the Israelites, not the Gentiles. The woman, however, refused to take 'no' for an answer. Three times she asked - in fact she begged! - and three times Jesus refused. But *still* the woman persisted, asking a fourth time. How did Jesus respond to her fourth request? We read:

> "Then Jesus said to her, "Woman, you have great faith! Your request is granted." And her daughter was healed at that moment." (Matthew 15:28)

What an extraordinary encounter! It was a real-life example of the parable of the persistent widow. In fact, it is uncanny how similar this real-life incident was to the parable. For instance, at one point, the disciples said to Jesus:

> "Lord, send her away, because she keeps crying out to us!" (Verse 23).

Just like the widow in the parable, the Canaanite woman would not take 'no' for an answer. She was loud, brash, insistent and persistent, continually crying out for help despite having her request denied three times. She would not go away! And, finally, Jesus commended her for her *"great faith"* and granted her request!

This incident raises all sorts of questions. Did Jesus always intend to heal the woman's daughter, but was just waiting to see how great her faith was? Or did the woman's persistence actually change the mind of Jesus? And, if the latter is true, what does this say about the relationship between prayer and the will of God? The Bible does not give us any clear answers (although I would oppose any theology that undermines the truth of God's absolute sovereignty). One thing is abundantly clear, however: if the Canaanite woman had given up after the first or second or even third rejection, her request would not have been granted. Her request was only granted because she *persisted*.

Jesus urges us to do likewise: to *"pray and not give up"* (Luke 18:1) and to *"cry out to God day and night"* (Luke 18:7) until our prayers are answered, too.

I must reiterate the necessary conditions for answered prayer that were mentioned in the previous chapter: praying in the will of God, in right relationship with Jesus and without blatant, unconfessed sin in our lives. But providing these things are in place - providing our prayers are selfless kingdom prayers, offered from a penitent heart of faith - we are urged to pray with a tenacious, dogged persistence for as long as it takes, until the answer arrives.

This is certainly the kind of persistence that the Apostle Paul demonstrated in his own prayer life. In the opening chapter of his letter to the church in Rome, he writes:

> "God is my witness ... how constantly I remember you in my prayers at all times" (Romans 1:9-10)

What is particularly impressive about this is the fact that Paul had not yet been to Rome, so he had not yet even met the church there. Despite this, he says he prays for them *"constantly ... in my prayers at all times"*. What remarkable faithfulness and persistence! This is the kind of faithful persistence that the Bible urges upon every Christian.

HOW TO DEVELOP A MORE CONSISTENT AND PERSISTENT PRAYER LIFE

Here are five practical suggestions:

1. READ GOD'S WORD

The more you read God's Word, the more you will want to pray. Reading God's Word will strengthen your faith and inspire you. It will increase your faith in the goodness and greatness of God – both of which are concepts that are foundational for anyone who would approach God in prayer. Reading the Bible will increase your desire to pray as you are reminded of God's powerful interventions throughout history and as your mind is drawn to the central values of his kingdom. Show me a Christian who is not praying, and I can almost guarantee that they aren't reading their Bible either.

How is your daily Bible reading going? Is it happening at all? Make a fresh commitment, right now, to start each day reading from God's Word. Decide, right now, what book you will start reading tomorrow.

I use a Bible reading app on my iPad (called Olive Tree) which allows me to bookmark my reading each day. It also has Greek and Hebrew, study notes and many commentaries available at the touch of a finger. Very helpful! There are many other practical apps and tools that are available to help you develop a regular Bible reading habit: daily Bible reading notes from Scripture Union, the One Year Bible, the Daily Bible, etc.

I usually read my Bible first thing in the morning, before I watch the morning news headlines on TV or look at emails or engage with anything else. It is a discipline I have set myself, because I want the first thing that enters my mind each day to be God's Word.

What about you? Is this a commitment you need to make too?

2. KEEP A PRAYER LIST OR A PRAYER JOURNAL

One way of increasing your consistency and persistence in prayer is to keep a list of things and people you are praying for. Perhaps you have done this in the past, but it has 'slipped off your radar' recently. Why not start again? Take a few moments now to write a list of all the things you should be praying for regularly, then divide them into days of the week. Spend some time praying for some of them right now!

I keep my prayer lists on my iPad and phone; a different list for each day. I pray immediately after my morning Bible reading. I read my Bible as I eat my muesli and then I pray. It's not a difficult thing to do if you set up a regular morning habit like this.

I have also kept a prayer journal in the past. This is an excellent way of keeping track of how and when God answers your prayers. Simply make a journal entry with a date whenever you start praying for something new, then write down the date of the answer and its details when it eventually is given. Looking back over your prayer journal is incredibly inspiring and encouraging as you see how often and how graciously God has answered your prayers.

3. SHARE ANSWERS TO PRAYER WITH OTHERS

When God does answer your prayers, don't keep it to yourself. Share it with others so that they can be encouraged and inspired in their own prayer life. This will also reinforce the efficacy of prayer in your own mind.

4. PRAY WITH OTHERS

If you struggle to be motivated to pray, you may find that praying with others will help. The prayers of others will inspire your own prayer life, and the regularity of meeting with them will help you to develop consistency in your own prayer life.

If you are married, what about praying with your spouse? This is often something that falls away when your prayer life becomes jaded or even non-existent. My wife and I have started praying together regularly again after several years where it was very spasmodic. We now try to pray together on a Sunday, after listening to an online sermon. We also pray occasionally immediately after dinner, before we get up from the table to wash the dishes. We do this when there are specific issues or urgent needs that have come to our attention throughout the course of the day. Obviously, if you have young children, then praying at the table immediately after dinner won't be the best time for significant prayer for you as a couple, but it could be an excellent time to engage in family prayer with your children.

5. DARE TO PRAY WITH GREATER BOLDNESS AND FAITH

Perhaps one reason why some Christians lack motivation to pray consistently and persistently is that they have never really seen God a 'big' answer to prayer – perhaps because they've never asked for one. Don't be afraid to ask God for big things, if you believe it is in accordance with his will.

1 Kings 17 records the amazing story of the first person to be raised from the dead in the Bible. The prophet Elijah had been lodging with a widow, and the widow's son became sick and died. The widow was understandably devastated and asked Elijah to do something about it. So, Elijah carried the dead boy into an upstairs room, laid him on a bed and then prostrated himself and cried out to God, *"Lord, my God, let this boy's life return to him!"* (v.21) Amazingly, the next verse tells us, *"The Lord heard Elijah's cry, and the boy's life returned to him, and he lived"* (v.22).

What is truly extraordinary about this incident, is that Elijah had no precedent upon which to base his prayer. Never before in the history of the world had someone been raised from the dead! Elijah didn't have a Bible with stories of people being raised from the dead upon which to base his prayer. This was the very first case of someone being brought back to life in the history of our world. It was brand new territory.

Elijah's prayer was a crazy, 'out-there' kind of prayer. He was asking God for something that had never been seen. He was asking for the impossible. If I had been Elijah's assistant, I would have been tugging his sleeve and whispering, *"Elijah, maybe you should tone that prayer down a bit. Back it down a few levels, buddy! Maybe just pray for the widow's comfort. Because if God doesn't answer your prayer for her son, her faith will be shot!"*

But Elijah dared to pray for the seemingly impossible.

Now, I can only assume that he was prompted by the Holy Spirit to pray this, and that is an extremely important point. He was clearly praying within the will of God - a point I have already stressed several times. But I wonder how often our prayers are limited by our inability to believe God for great things. Do you dare to pray big prayers for your church? For your community? For yourself and your loved ones?

6. A PRACTICAL TOOL

If a protracted time of daily prayer seems a bit daunting to you, why not start with the old A.C.T.S. formula? Start by spending just one minute each morning on each of the key elements of prayer: Adoration, Confession, Thanksgiving and Supplication. Supplication has two distinct sub-elements: Intercession (praying for others) and Petition (praying for your own needs and issues). This means that there are 5 key elements of prayer. Spending just one minute each day on each of these 5 elements is a good way to kick start your renewed prayer life. I call it the "The 5 Minute Prayer Challenge":

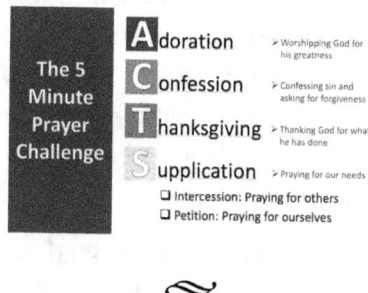

PERSONAL REFLECTION

How persistent are you in your own prayer life? Realistically, how often in a week do you pray for more than a minute or two? How can you change this? Is there a set time each day when you can devote some time to prayer, so that you can be a "persistent" pray-er?

How persistent are you in terms of the CONTENT of your prayers? God calls us to "pray and not give up". Are there people or issues that you really ought to be praying for every day or at least every week? As I've already suggested, make a list of those people or issues and make a fresh commitment to pray for them more regularly.

Pray for them now!

If you are keen to begin praying more consistently, and you think a daily prayer list would be beneficial, keeping that list on your phone or some other device could be a helpful way of ensuring that you persistently pray for the people and issues that need your prayers. Why not give that a try?

Do you pray regularly with your husband /wife? This is often one of the things that drops away when your prayer life is sliding. Make a fresh commitment to pray with your partner. When would be a good time to do this? Perhaps in bed at night doesn't work for you. What about at the dinner table immediately after dinner? If you have children, perhaps some other time?

GROUP DISCUSSION QUESTIONS

1. Share your thoughts and impressions from this chapter. What was new to you? What was helpful? Is there anything you are still unsure about?

Read Luke 18:1-8

2. Do you think we sometimes *"pray and give up"*? Are there examples from your own life that you feel comfortable sharing?

3. Read verses 3-5 again. Notice the widow's incredible persistence. She *"kept coming to him"* despite the fact that the unjust judge was not really interested in helping her. The widow displayed an incredibly focussed desperation and determination. How could we display the same determination and persistence in our prayers?

4. Read verses 7-8 again. Jesus promises that God will grant the requests of those who are persistent in prayer. But notice, in verse 7, that he is only promising to do this for those *"who cry out to him day and night"*. Apart from frequency of praying, what

attitude does that phrase also indicate? How can we begin to pray like that?

5. Verse 8 says that God *"will see that they get justice, and quickly."* How does this align with the fact that many of us have things we have been praying about for many years which are still unanswered?

Read Matthew 15:21-28

6. Notice Jesus' three initial refusals of the woman's request: verses 23 (where Jesus refuses to even reply), 24 and 26. Read these verses out again. Why does Jesus initially refuse her?

7. Read verse 28. It is only after the woman has continued to ask (a fourth time!), choosing to persist despite three initial refusals, that Jesus finally grants her request. Notice that Jesus commends her for her *"great faith"*. How is her persistence a sign of "great faith"? Isn't she just stubborn?

8. Did this woman change Jesus' mind? Does this mean that our persistent prayers can change God's mind? How does this work?

9. Read through the "5 Minute Prayer Challenge" at the end of this chapter. Refresh your memory about what each of the elements of prayer in the A.C.T.S. acronym represent. As a group, pray through that acronym now, spending a couple of minutes on each element of prayer. You may need to be sensitive when you come to the element of confession, perhaps just acknowledging your need for forgiveness generally, without feeling the need to unveil your deepest, darkest failings to everyone! It would be helpful to gather some prayer points before you begin.

PART III

CONNECTING WITH GOD'S WORD

9

TRUST THE BIBLE'S RELIABILITY

If prayer is the breath of the soul, God's Word is food for the soul. When we read the Bible, God speaks to us and our souls are nourished. If we are to connect with God and continue to deepen our connection with him, reading his Word is extremely important. Regular Bible reading will strengthen your faith, convict you of sin, shape your character and instruct you in the path of salvation. This is why Paul exhorted the young Pastor, Timothy, to continue reading Holy Scripture:

> *"But as for you, continue in what you have learned and have become convinced of, because you know those from whom you learned it, and how from infancy you have known the Holy Scriptures, which are able to make you wise for salvation through faith in Christ Jesus. All Scripture is God-breathed and is useful for teaching, rebuking, correcting and training in righteousness, so that the servant of God may be thoroughly equipped for every good work." (2 Timothy 3:14-17)*

But there is a crisis of trust in the Bible in some branches of the church today. Liberal Christians claim that the Bible's transmission down through the ages has been flawed, marred by human error, and that many uninspired human teachings have crept into its narrative. Liberals claim that we can't trust the Bible's textual fidelity and that we can't accept its teachings at face value.

So, before I implore you to read the Bible regularly, I firstly need to defend its veracity. You need to be assured that it is, indeed, God's inspired Word, completely authoritative and without error.

Let me begin by explaining the process of textual transmission – how the Bible has come down to us through the ages.

THE METICULOUS COPYING PROCESS OF THE SCRIBES

While it is true that, for most of its long life, the Bible was copied by hand, the claim that a vast number of errors must have crept into the text ignores the extremely rigorous copying process that was instituted by the Jews. In ancient times, the copying of the Old Testament was the sole task of professional scribes. The Jews revered their sacred text so highly that the copying process was conducted according to the strictest possible guidelines.

When a copy of a book of the Old Testament became worn or faded and a new copy was ordered, a single scribe was given the task of producing the new copy. Working from the original scroll, the scribe would copy the first word of the first line, then he would put down his writing quill and pick up a pointer, called a yad. Using the yad, he would count the number of letters, jots and tittles (small grammatical marks) in the original word and then count the number of letters, jots and tittles in the newly copied word, to ensure that the word had been copied exactly. If the new word was correct, he would put down his yad, pick up his quill and copy the second word. The second word's letters, jots and tittles would then be counted and verified using the yad. This process continued for each word, individually, on the first line. When every word of the first line had been successfully copied and verified, a second verification process then took place. The scribe would take up the yad and count every letter, jot and tittle in the entire first line of the original scroll and then undertake the same count in the first line of the new scroll. This second verification ensured that the scribe had not missed an entire word in the copying process.

This copying and verification process continued word by word and line by line, until the first page of the scroll had been completed. (Hebrew scrolls consisted of many individual pages glued together into one continuous scroll). When the last line of the first page had been successfully copied and verified, a third verification process was then undertaken. Using the yad, the scribe would then count every letter, jot and tittle on the *entire* original page and then would undertake the same count on the new copy, to verify that the pages were exactly the same. This ensured that the scribe had not missed copying an entire line and it also provided a final verification of the entire page. If the scribe was satisfied that the copied page was identical to the original, a second scribe then had to undertake the same count in order to corroborate the verification. Only once this final verification by a second scribe had taken place was the new page accepted as accurate and it could be glued onto the new scroll. The scribe could then proceed to begin copying the next page. If, at any point, a copying error was detected on a page, even if it was a single missed letter in the last word on the page, Jewish law dictated that the entire page had to be burnt, and the copying of that page had to be recommenced. This rigorous process continued throughout the entire scroll until the final page had been copied and verified.

Historians acknowledge that this rigorous copying process is the most meticulous copying process in human history. In no other culture, at no other time, was the copying of documents undertaken with such obsessively meticulous attention to detail. Sceptics who claim that the Bible must be full of copying errors simply have not bothered to investigate the process by which it was copied.

The Dead Sea Scrolls

Despite the meticulous copying process of Hebrew scribes being well known among historians, sceptics continued to claim, throughout the first half of the 20th century, that gross errors must have crept into the Hebrew Scriptures over the centuries. They claimed that we can have no way of knowing that what we read today was anything like what was originally written. The discovery of the Dead Sea Scrolls, however, silenced their accusations.

The Dead Sea Scrolls are a collection of approximately 1,000 documents, written in Hebrew, Aramaic and Greek, discovered between 1947 and 1979 in caves near Qumran on the shores of the Dead Sea, 18km East of Jerusalem and 500m below sea level.

The first manuscripts were found by a shepherd who threw a rock into a cave to chase out a goat that had strayed. When he did so, he heard the sound of breaking pottery, and went to investigate. The cave contained a collection of sealed pottery jars. Inside the jars were ancient documents wrapped in linen to preserve them.

There are 11 caves which were subsequently explored. Most historians believe that the caves were the monastic retreat of a Jewish Essene community (a Jewish sect) who had apparently retreated there during or shortly before the Roman purge of

Israel around 70 AD. The majority of documents in the caves were parchment (animal skin) with a few papyrus documents as well. These documents represent the library of the ancient Essene community who lived there. Cave 4, where 80% of the manuscripts were found, contained approximately 15,000 fragments (some of them very small) from 500 documents.

The documents range in date from 200 BC to about 68 AD, and include Biblical and non-Biblical books. The non-Biblical books include commentaries on the Old Testament, hymns, liturgies, accounts, monastic rules and procedures. The Biblical books comprise copies of about half the books in the Old Testament, including a copy of Isaiah which is 1000 years older than any previously discovered copy! In fact, the Dead Sea Scrolls are, to this day, the oldest collection of Old Testament books ever found.

The Dead Sea Scrolls are important because:

1. They bring us hundreds of years closer to the Old Testament autographs (the original documents, penned by the authors).

2. They show how little the Old Testament documents have changed over time. For example, they reveal that the copy of the book of Isaiah, found among the Dead Sea Scrolls, when compared with the previously earliest existing copy (1,000 years later) was almost identical – the only differences being minor variations in spelling. The Old Testament remained unchanged through all the many centuries of its copying!

The Dead Sea Scrolls have been hailed by most archaeologists as the greatest archaeological discovery of the 20th century. For Christians, they have provided unarguable, objective proof of the textual reliability of the Old Testament and the accuracy of the transmission process over the millennia.

THE OVERWHELMING DOCUMENTARY EVIDENCE FOR THE NEW TESTAMENT

The copying of the New Testament was not always undertaken with such meticulous rigour as was the Old Testament. While some copies of New Testament books were produced by professional scribes, many were copied by ordinary people. This was because the new Christian movement was ostracised from Judaism, and it quickly became what we would call today a house church movement. Thus, when Paul wrote a letter to a particular church in a particular city, his letter was so highly valued that every household in the church wanted a copy. The original document was often passed around from household to household, and each household made their own copy. Eventually letters to specific cities and churches found their way to other cities, as Christians around the world were eager to read the letters from Paul and the other Apostles. In this way, hundreds and even thousands of copies were produced all around the ancient world. Those who produced the new copies were not usually trained scribes, but were ordinary people, like you and me, with varying literary abilities. This often resulted in incidental copying errors. Words were misspelt. Words were occasionally omitted. Sometimes a whole line was accidently skipped. If a flawed copy was then passed on and copied, these errors were perpetuated in subsequent copies, and so errors tended to accumulate.

While this might seem extremely problematic, the vast number of surviving copies of these ancient New Testament documents allows textual critics to examine the varying versions (known as variants) of a New Testament passage and ascertain, to within a very high degree of certainty, the exact wording of the original text. Textual critics are like textual detectives who piece together the wording of the autographic (original) text. In most cases this is relatively easy to do. Using dating techniques, textual critics can trace document families back through time, identifying when variants (mistakes) were introduced to the text and arriving at the precise wording of the original text via corroboration with other similarly aged texts.

An example might help to illustrate. In Ephesians 5:31 there are four variants among the surviving manuscripts:

1. "For this reason a man leaves his father and mother and clings to *his* wife"

2. "For this reason a man leaves his father and mother and clings to *the* wife"

3. "For this reason a man leaves his father and mother and *joins* the wife"

4. "For this reason a man leaves his father and mother".

Using dating techniques and comparing the textual family lines of each of these variants, textual critics can determine which of these variants was the original text and can even determine, to within a decade or two, when each of the variants was introduced to the textual record. Accordingly, it is the first version that is recognised as autographic (from the pen of the author) and is published in our modern Bibles.

Compared to other books of antiquity, no other literary work comes close to approaching the New Testament in terms of manuscript evidence and close time-span between the autograph (the original document) and the earliest extant copies (copies still in existence). The table below reveals how extraordinarily well-attested the New Testament is when compared to other ancient works. Note the extremely small time-gap between the date of the original writing and the date of the earliest surviving copies of the New Testament. Note, also, the extraordinary number of surviving Greek manuscripts of the

New Testament, which allows scholars to ascertain the exact wording of the original texts with great accuracy.

Author	Date Written	Earliest Surviving Copy	Time Span between original & surviving copy	No. of Copies
Pliny	61-113 A.D.	850 A.D.	750 yrs	7
Plato	427-347 B.C.	900 A.D.	1200 yrs	7
Demosthenes	4th Cent. B.C.	1100 A.D.	800 yrs	8
Herodotus	480-425 B.C.	900 A.D.	1300 yrs	8
Suetonius	75-160 A.D.	950 A.D.	800 yrs	8
Thucydides	460-400 B.C.	900 A.D.	1300 yrs	8
Euripides	480-406 B.C.	1100 A.D.	1300 yrs	9
Aristophanes	450-385 B.C.	900 A.D.	1200 yrs	10
Caesar	100-44 B.C.	900 A.D.	1000 yrs	10
Tacitus	100 A.D.	1100 A.D.	1000 yrs	20
Aristotle	384-322 B.C.	1100 A.D.	1400 yrs	49
Sophocles	496-406 B.C.	1000 A.D.	1400 yrs	193
Homer (Iliad)	900 B.C.	400 B.C.	500 yrs	643
New Testament	50-100 A.D.	c. 115 - 135 A.D.	15-40 yrs	5600 Greek MS

This extraordinary manuscript attestation of the New Testament, together with the temporal proximity of surviving manuscripts to the autographs, is unparalleled in ancient literature. This allows textual critics to arrive at the precise original wording of each verse of the Bible with an extremely high degree of certainty.

The Bible, as a reliable historical document, stands head and shoulders above all other literary works from antiquity. We can have great confidence that the words we read today are, indeed, the words that were originally penned by the authors. The claim of liberal Christians that the transmission of the Bible is not trustworthy, simply doesn't stand up to academic scrutiny.

But that is not the only claim made by liberal Christians. Some liberals also maintain that many of the events and people described in the Bible are purely fanciful. According to these critics, even if the words we have in the Bible today are the original words, they cannot be taken literally, because the writers were often merely concocting religious myths rather than recording real human history. In other words, they claim that many of the people and events recorded in the Bible were not real: they were simply made-up stories.

If we are to read the Bible with any degree of certainty, this claim must also be dealt with. But is there any way of validating the Bible's extraordinary story?

HISTORICAL CORROBORATION OF BIBLICAL EVENTS AND PEOPLE

The difficulty we face is that the books of the Bible were written between 2,000 and 4,500 years ago. When studying ANYTHING from those ancient times, historians often have scant corroborative evidence to work with. The Bible is not alone in this. Time and the natural processes of weathering and decay assure that very few documents and artifacts have survived intact, particularly from the very early periods of Old testament history. Despite this, archaeological digs over the last century have uncovered a steady stream of corroborating evidence for the biblical narrative. Here are just a few examples:

- The Old Testament patriarchs, Abraham, Isaac, Jacob and Moses, were once thought (by liberals) to be entirely fictitious, because no mention of them had ever been found in other ancient historical documents. Some people might say that it doesn't matter whether the patriarchs were real people or simply mythical, as it is the meaning behind their stories that is important. But this is not the case. The life stories of the patriarchs are the foundation on which the historical record of the Bible is based. If they are mere myths, how can we trust anything that the Bible says? Furthermore, the New Testament writers clearly refer to them as real people, and they appear in the genealogies of Jesus as his ancestors. Fortunately, the issue was resolved in a series of archaeological digs between 1925 and 1931 at Nuzi, near the city of Asshur (in Iraq). A series of clay tablets were discovered which not only confirmed the patriarchs as historical figures, but also corroborated many other important details in the book of Genesis.

- The Old Testament contains numerous references to Israel's conflict with the Assyrians, but for many years there was no evidence outside of the Bible that the ancient Assyrian empire even existed. Sceptics therefore claimed that this was an example of the Bible's fanciful nature. But archaeological digs at the site of ancient Nineveh in the early 1900's uncovered many clay tablets describing the Assyrian empire and culture in great detail, including the names of key people who are recorded in the Bible.

- Until the beginning of the 20th century, the Hittites were unknown outside of the Bible, and historians had long claimed that this was another example of the Bible's fanciful nature. However, in 1906, a Hittite city was uncovered east of Ankara, Turkey, along with clay tablets containing writing that provides detailed descriptions of the Hittite culture and even their dealings with the ancient Israelites.

- For many years, sceptics asserted that King David, who figures prominently in the Bible, was a myth. No other records of him had ever been found. This was supposedly further 'proof' that the Bible was a fable. But in 1993 a group of archaeologists digging in northern Galilee found clay tablets with inscriptions from the ninth century BC, providing details of King David's life and reign. The discovery was sensational enough to make the front page of the New York Times.

To date there are literally hundreds of similar stories of archaeological finds confirming the people and events of the Bible. Professor Walter Kaiser, in his book entitled, *The Old Testament Documents: Are They Reliable and Relevant?*, wrote:

> "Biblical archaeology has greatly enhanced the study of the biblical texts and their history. Archaeological discoveries have consistently provided uncanny confirmation of Old Testament persons, peoples and places." (2001, p.97).

In his book, *Biblical Archaeology: Factual Evidence to Support the Historicity of the Bible*, Dr Paul L. Maier writes,

> "Ever since scientific archaeology started a century and a half ago, the consistent pattern has been this: the hard evidence from the ground has borne out the biblical record again and again — and again. The Bible has nothing to fear from the spade." [1]

Of course, it is one thing to corroborate the existence of biblical people and places, it is quite another matter to confirm the Bible's account of miracles. Liberals are particularly sceptical regarding the miracles recorded in the Bible. They claim that even if the people and places mentioned in the Bible are historically accurate, the accounts of miracles must surely be fabricated, because everyone knows that miracles aren't possible!

In attempting to verify biblical accounts of miracles, we are faced with the problem that the nature of many of the reported miracles is such that there is no possible means of verification. For instance, when God spoke to people or manifested himself in the world in a physical way, such as the burning bush or the pillars of cloud and fire in the book of Exodus, these interventions would not have left any tangible evidence.

Occasionally, however, the miracles are of such a nature that we could expect to find some evidence remaining. And that is exactly what we do find. The miraculous collapse of the walls of Jericho is a case in point. The Bible describes how the walls of the city crumbled after God commanded his people to march around the city blowing trumpets. This, of course, was greeted with ridicule by the sceptic community until an archaeological dig by Dame Kathleen Kenyon in the 1950s discovered that the walls of ancient Jericho had all collapsed OUTWARD rather than INWARD as would be the case if they had been battered down by a besieging army. The excavation and study of these ancient outwardly-collapsed walls documented a number of highly technical findings which corroborated the biblical account of their demise with stunningly precise details.

Another recent archaeological corroboration of a biblical miracle was the identification of the mountain Jabal Maqla as the biblical Mount Sinai. What is particularly fascinating about Jabal Maqla is that the entire top of the mountain is blackened, with rocks that have obviously melted, as if the summit has been scorched by some kind of intense fire. The rocks have a glassy black surface but when they are broken open, they reveal themselves to be red granite. Some kind of intense heat has been applied to the mountain top (which was never a volcano) that has literally melted the surface of the rocks. This extraordinary geological evidence accords with the Bible's description that God "descended on it in fire" and that the entire top of the mountain was like "a furnace" as the Israelites, led by Moses, camped around it.

CORROBORATION OF THE MIRACLES OF JESUS

The miracles of Jesus are the greatest point of attack for those wishing to deny the historical reliability of the Bible. Jesus' list of miracles is extraordinary:

- On three separate occasions he raised dead people to life.

- On one of those occasions, Jesus stopped a funeral procession in the street and raised the dead person.

- On another of those occasions, the person he raised to life had been dead for three days.

- He instantly healed a wide range of diseases including leprosy and blindness.

- He instantly healed paraplegics and quadriplegics.

- He multiplied a small amount of food to feed thousands.

- He changed water into wine.

- He walked on water.

Sceptics have long held that miracles are not scientifically possible and that Jesus' followers must, therefore, have invented these myths to give credence to their new religion. Fortunately, there is overwhelming historical evidence which corroborates Jesus as a miracle worker.

For starters, the Jewish first century historian, Flavius Josephus, describes Jesus as *"a worker of wonders"* in his book, *The Antiqui-*

ties of the Jews. This phrase was a common first century term for describing occurrences of a supernatural or miraculous nature. This description of Jesus as a miracle worker is particularly impressive, as it comes from the pen of Josephus – a traditional Jew who was not a Christian.

Even more impressive is the acknowledgment in the Jewish Talmud of Jesus' miracles. The Talmud is one of the sacred texts of the Judaism; a companion sacred text to the Torah. Significantly, it was being written at the time of Jesus, at the same time that Jesus was living and ministering in Judea and Galilee. As well as offering reflections and commentary on the teachings of the Torah, the scribes who were writing the Talmud also often reflected on current events within their society. Thus, we find eleven separate references to Jesus and his miracles within the narrative of the Talmud. This is because Jesus was the biggest story of the day. His miracles were the talk of the whole nation!

Significantly, the Jewish scribes who were writing the Talmud did not deny the fact of his miracles, even though the Jews were Jesus' enemies. They could not deny his miracles because they were so obvious and so well-attested, often witnessed by thousands of people. Instead, the scribes attributed his miracles to the power of the devil. Thus, the Talmud repeatedly refers to him as a "sorcerer".

For instance, in BT, Sanhedrin 43a of the Talmud, we read,

> "On the eve of the Passover Yeshua [the Nazarene] was hanged. For forty days before the execution took place a herald went forth and cried, 'He is going forth to be stoned because he has practiced sorcery and enticed Israel to apostasy. Anyone who can say anything in his favour, let him come and plead on his behalf.' And

> since nothing was brought forward in his favour, he was hanged on the eve of Passover."[2]

Even Jesus' enemies – the ones who eventually had him put to death – could not deny his miracles. In the Talmud, they left us with extremely strong historical corroboration of his miracle working power. This is referred to by historians as 'corroboration by hostile witnesses' and is considered to be corroboration of the highest order.

The historical evidence for the veracity of Jesus' miracles is so strong that even the famous liberal scholar, Rudolf Bultmann, conceded:

> "But there can be no doubt that Jesus did such deeds, which were, in his and his contemporaries' understanding, miracles, that is, deeds that were the result of supernatural, divine causality. Doubtless he healed the sick and cast out demons." (Rudolf Bultmann, Jesus, Berlin: Deutsche Bibliothek, 1926, p. 159.)

The Bible is a trustworthy book. It has been copied and transcribed down through the ages with meticulous attention to detail. Its words are completely reliable and its text is unchanged.

Furthermore, the people, places and events that are recorded within its narrative are continually being corroborated as archaeology uncovers more evidence. In particular, we can have great confidence that the miracles recorded in the Bible really did happen. The Bible is an accurate record of God's supernatural dealings with mankind.

But is the Bible more than a mere history book? It is one thing to say that it is factual and reliable, but is it more than just an accurate record of biblical history? The Bible claims to be more than a history book. It claims to be the living Word of God – a message from God himself that is capable of transforming lives. Is there any evidence for this extraordinary claim?

That is the topic of the next chapter.

∼

PERSONAL REFLECTION

Have you had doubts about the veracity and reliability of the Bible? Perhaps you have been influenced by liberal claims of errors and mistakes in the Bible. God is calling you to trust his Word and to trust him, the one who has overseen and protected its transmission to us, down through the ages.

GROUP DISCUSSION QUESTIONS

1. Share your thoughts and impressions from this chapter. What was new to you? What was helpful? Is there anything you are still unsure about?

Read 2 Peter 1:16-21

2. In verses 16-18, Peter is dealing with the accusation by sceptics in the first century that the stories about Jesus were "cleverly devised stories"; in other words, myths. Peter refutes this accusation by pointing to some clear evidence in verses 16-18. What is that evidence?

3. In verses 19-21, Peter is dealing with the more general disbelief in the reliability of the Christian scriptures as a whole. He begins his refutation by simply stating that *"the prophetic message"* (inspired scripture recorded by God's prophets) is *"completely reliable"* (verse 19). In verses 20-21, what does he then claim about the Christian scriptures?

Read Matthew 24:36-39

4. In this passage, Jesus is drawing a comparison between his future return to Earth and the flood of Noah in the ancient past. What parallels does he make?

5. This comparison by Jesus indicates that he believes in Noah as a real historical person and in the flood as a real historical event. How should this influence our attitude toward the stories in the Bible, including the Old Testament?

Read Luke 21:33

6. This is an extremely strong statement by Jesus, indicating that he will ensure that his words will never disappear from the historical record. How does this refute the claim by liberal Christians and sceptics that the transmission of the Bible has been so unreliable throughout the ages that we can no longer be sure exactly what Jesus said or did?

7. What does the liberal view of the Bible's unreliability reveal about their concept of God?

Read Isaiah 40:8

8. Explain this promise in your own words.

9. **Read the following verses from Psalm 119, and discover the common theme.** (Perhaps get different members of the group to read out different verses):

Verse 89

Verse 91

Verse 111

Verse 138

Verse 140

Verse 142

Verse 152

Verse 160

Read Psalm 119:105

10. How is God's word a lamp and a light? How does it function in this way? Explain.

Read Joshua 1:7-8

11. As Joshua is about to lead the Israelites into the promised land and face the perilous task of doing battle with the inhabitants as agents of God's judgment, God gives him final instructions. Significantly, God does not discuss battle tactics or leadership strategies. Instead he focuses on the necessity for Joshua to immerse himself in God's Word. Why do you think this is?

12. In these two verses there are commands and promises. What are the commands or exhortations regarding how Joshua is to treat God's Word?

13. What blessings will flow to Joshua (and us!) if he does this?

10

TRUST THE BIBLE'S INSPIRATION

As the Apostle Paul neared the end of his life, he found himself imprisoned for a second time in Rome, under the Emperor Nero. In contrast to his first imprisonment, when he had lived in a private house and was well cared for, he was now locked away in a cold dungeon, chained to a wall like a common criminal. His supporters had difficulty locating him, and his health was deteriorating. Realising that his life was nearing its end, he wrote one final letter, giving encouragement and instructions to a struggling young pastor in the church at Ephesus. Mid-way through that letter, as he sought to exhort Timothy to persevere through various difficulties, Paul reflected on the many ordeals he had suffered in his own service for Christ and reaffirmed his absolute faith in the inspired nature of Holy Scripture:

> "You, however, know all about my teaching, my way of life, my purpose, faith, patience, love, endurance, persecutions, sufferings – what kinds of things happened to me in Antioch, Iconium and Lystra, the persecutions I endured. Yet the Lord rescued me from them all.... As for you, continue in what you have learned and have

> become convinced of, because you know those from whom you learned it, and how from infancy you have known the Holy Scriptures, which are able to make you wise for salvation through faith in Christ Jesus. All Scripture is God-breathed and is useful for teaching, rebuking, correcting and training in righteousness, so that all God's people may be thoroughly equipped for every good work." (2 Timothy 3:10-17).

To his dying day, to his final breath, the Apostle Paul was convinced that the book we now call "the Bible" is God's inspired, authoritative message to mankind. His assertion that it is *"holy"* and *"God-breathed"* could not be clearer.

As a Bible-believing Christian, I uphold a high view of Holy Scripture. This collection of ancient writings does not represent the mere speculations of flawed human beings; it bears the stamp of God's Spirit. It is much more than a mere history book: it is alive with the breath of God. My belief in the divinely inspired nature of the Bible, however, does not rest upon mere blind faith. My confidence regarding its inspiration rests upon some very convincing evidence; both objective and subjective.

THE BIBLE'S MIRACULOUS INTERNAL CONSISTENCY

The Bible was written over a period of approximately 1,600 years, by over 40 different authors from a diversity of cultures, backgrounds and languages. Yet, despite this, it exhibits an internal consistency that is beyond remarkable – it is miraculous! During my school teaching years, I often said to my Biblical Studies classes that if I sent them to watch a football match and each student had to subsequently write a report of the match, the resulting collage of reports would almost certainly contain discrepancies, inconsistencies and contradictions. Such is our fallible human nature. But the Bible contains no such gross inconsistencies. Despite the diversity of authorship and time periods, the Bible speaks with a cohesive, unified voice. This is only possible because of the miraculous inspiration of the Holy Spirit as he guided the writers to record God's message to mankind. The remarkable internal consistency of the Bible is the first piece of evidence that supports the inspired nature of the Bible.

FULFILLED PROPHECY WITHIN THE BIBLE

A more impressive area of evidence for the Bible's inspired nature is the many fulfilled prophecies that it contains. In his *"Encyclopedia of Biblical Prophecy"* [2], J. Barton Payne lists 1,817 predictive prophecies in the Bible. While some of these are still awaiting fulfilment, as they are predictions regarding the final events of human history, the rest were fulfilled in precise detail, often centuries after their prediction. 191 of these prophecies are messianic, foretelling specific details of the long-awaited Messiah. They predicted the precise nature of Christ's birth, ministry, death and resurrection, centuries before Christ was born. For example:

- 700 years before Christ, Isaiah made the seemingly outrageous prediction that the Messiah would be born to a virgin (Isaiah 7:14).

- Isaiah also predicted the messiah's rejection and death at the hands of the Jewish leaders (Isaiah 53).

- 650 years before Christ, Micah predicted that the Messiah would be born in Bethlehem (Micah 5:2).

- Moses, writing 1,500 years before Christ, predicted that he would be from the tribe of Judah (Genesis 49:10).

- Even more remarkably, Psalm 22 predicted Christ's

death by crucifixion, including the piercing of his hands and feet, yet this was written centuries before the Romans had even invented crucifixion!

Other extraordinary predictions include:

- The piercing of the Messiah's side with a spear (Zech 12:10).

- The casting of lots for his clothing (Psalm 22:18).

- The 30 pieces of silver paid to Judas to betray the Messiah (Zech 11:12-13).

- The fact that Jesus would be beaten and spat upon (Micah 5:1 and Isaiah 50:6)

- That Jesus would be given wine vinegar to drink as he died (Psalm 69:21).

- That Jesus would be buried in a rich man's tomb (Isaiah 53:9).

- Another extraordinary prediction is found in the book of Daniel which predicted the exact year of Christ's death, centuries before the event. In Daniel 9:24-26, the angel Gabriel appears to Daniel and prophecies that the Messiah will be put to death 483 years after the rebuilding of Jerusalem is commenced. The rebuilding of Jerusalem after the return from exile is thought to have occurred sometime around 450 to 460 BC, which would infer a crucifixion date of between 23 to 33 AD. Biblical scholars estimate, from historical records, that the most likely date of Christ's crucifixion is 27 AD, which fits perfectly with the prediction in the book of Daniel. Even more extraordinary is the fact that Daniel lived about 605 to 538 BC – nearly six hundred years before the birth of Christ!

These are just a small selection of the many hundreds of extraordinarily precise predictions in the Bible, made centuries before their eventual fulfilments. The probability of all these prophecies being fulfilled by random chance is a statistical impossibility. These fulfilled predictive prophecies of the Bible provide powerful evidence for the Bible's supernatural inspiration. God was clearly at work, inspiring the prophecies within the Bible's pages. He moved the writers, giving them supernatural insight into events way beyond the scope of their human vision. These extraordinary, fulfilled prophecies offer clear objective evidence, anchored in historical time and space, of the Bible's inspired nature. Isaiah 45:21-22 declares:

> "Who foretold this long ago? Who declared it from the distant past? Was it not I, the Lord? And there is no God apart from me: a righteous God and a Saviour. There is none but me. Turn to me and be saved, all you ends of the earth; for I am God, and there is no other."

THE BIBLE'S ABILITY TO TRANSFORM LIVES

But we have not yet plumbed the depths of the inspired nature of the Bible. Not only does it reveal a staggering supernatural knowledge of predicted events long before their fulfilment, it also claims to have an ongoing supernatural power to transform lives in the present. It is more than simply an inspired book of ancient history. The Bible claims to be the living voice of God to the world today, capable of bringing spiritual light and life to dry and barren souls.

> "The law of the Lord is perfect, reviving the soul; the testimony of the Lord is sure, making wise the simple; the precepts of the Lord are right, rejoicing the heart; the commandment of the Lord is pure, enlightening the eyes" (Psalm 19:7-8)

> "For the Word of God is living and active, sharper than any two-edged sword, dividing even between soul and spirit, joints and of marrow, and discerning the thoughts and intentions of the heart" (Hebrews 4:12).

> "All scripture is inspired by God, and is useful [effective] for teaching, rebuking, correcting and training in righteousness." (2 Timothy 3:16)

The Bible claims to be endowed with God's supernatural power to facilitate profound transformation in the lives of those who read it with an open heart. Millions of Christians testify that this claim has proven true in their own lives.

Of course, this is purely subjective evidence which most sceptics would scoff at, yet surely the fact that tens of millions of people testify to the Bible's life-changing power must be taken into account.

When I was the minister of a church in Coffs Harbour, New South Wales, in the 1990s, I encountered a man (for convenience I will refer to him as Phil – not his real name) who had been converted to Christ while in prison. Significantly, no other person played a part in his conversion. He simply found a Gideon's Bible in his prison cell and began reading it. As he read the Gospels and the books of the New Testament, he encountered God in a powerful way. God spoke to him, convicting Phil of his need for repentance and his need to turn to Christ in faith. There, in his lonely prison cell, the living Word of God convicted him and transformed him. He has since gone on to live his whole life for the Lord, becoming a missionary and taking the Gospel to those who have not yet heard of Christ.

Phil's story could be multiplied thousands of times. There are people all over the world who have encountered God powerfully in the pages of his Living Word and have had their lives transformed as a result.

I am one of those people! As I continue to read the Bible, I encounter God. His Spirit energises the words on each page and his voice whispers words of truth and life into my heart. My own daily, subjective experience affirms the Apostle Paul's ancient assertion that this book truly is *"God-breathed"*. Millions of Christians similarly testify to regularly, and at times, powerfully encountering God through his written Word. Minds are renewed, lives are transformed and destinies are irrevocably and eternally altered through the life-changing power of the Bible.

A MODERN CHALLENGE

Belief in the inspired nature of the Bible has direct implications for the practice of Christianity today. If the Bible truly is God's inspired Word, rather than merely the flawed teachings of fallible humans, then Christians ought to obey and follow its teachings, even if those teachings are increasingly unpopular within wider society.

Several years ago, Australia had a national plebiscite to determine whether to officially legalise same sex marriage. After the plebiscite I had several conversations with Christians who admitted that they voted "yes". When I asked them how they came to that decision, they said things like, *"I can't really see anything wrong with allowing homosexuals to be happy too."* When they asked me why I voted "no", I pointed to the clear teaching in the Bible that condemns homosexuality; from the repeated denunciation in Leviticus 18 and 20, to the unequivocal condemnation of the practice in Romans 1, which refers to it as "unnatural" and "detestable" and a "sin" in God's eyes. I asked these people how they responded to these and other passages, and they responded with comments like, *"It just doesn't seem right to call it a sin"* and *"Maybe those parts of the Bible don't apply to us today"*. One respondent simply said, *"Well, I disagree with the Bible on that issue."*

This is an increasingly common phenomenon. Many Christians now have a diminished view of the Bible. They regard it as partially outdated and containing ethics that no longer apply to our modern world. Of course, this is not a new claim. For over one hundred years, liberal 'Christians' have been claiming that the Bible is full of misguided human teachings and outdated ethics.

Many years ago, I preached a sermon about the inspiration and inerrancy of the Bible. I explained how some Christians regard some sections of the Bible as outdated and irrelevant. As I spoke, I started ripping pages and whole sections out of an old hymn book which I pretended was a Bible. I began to fling the ripped out pages into the air, saying things like, *"This bit's no good, let's get rid of that! And I don't agree with this bit, so let's rip that out too!"* Some members of the congregation were horrified that I was desecrating a 'Bible', but I explained to them that this is precisely what people are doing when they pick and choose which bits to believe and which bits to disregard.

The Bible claims that it is *entirely* inspired and authoritative. The Apostle Paul writes:

> "ALL scripture is inspired by God, and is useful for teaching, rebuking, correcting and training in righteousness" (2 Tim 3:16).

As an evangelical Christian I believe that the Bible is divinely inspired and timelessly authoritative in its entirety. It is God's Word, and God doesn't make mistakes.

This is an important point. How big is your view of God? Is the One you call God powerful enough to ensure that everything recorded for us in his Word is true? If you believe that the Bible is only partially inspired and true – that it also contains teachings that are biased, outdated, flawed and uninspired – then whoever it is you call 'God' is not really God at all, because he can't even get the publication of a single book right!

The God I believe in is the One who spoke a billion galaxies into existence with the command of his voice. He is the One who created the whole universe from nothing. He is the all-powerful, all-knowing, eternally-present God for whom nothing is impossible. Take a walk outside one night and look up at the stars in all their grandeur. The One who spoke the universe into existence has also spoken to us in his Word, and he is more than able to ensure that its message is as accurate and relevant today as it was when it was first written.

PERSONAL CHALLENGE

What about you? Do you believe in the inspired nature of God's Word? Do you believe that God has inspired and underpinned the writing of the Bible, and that it remains his message to mankind today?

This is not just an academic question. It has direct practical application for our lives; for the formation of our values and ethics. Upon what do you base your beliefs and ethics? Are they based upon the inspired, authoritative Word of God? Or are they dictated by the changeable whims of society and your own confused thinking? If you start discarding parts of the Bible because they are inconvenient or difficult, where do you stop? How do you decide which bits are acceptable and which bits are not? I believe in a Creator God who has communicated clearly and unequivocally with humanity through His Word (and, of course, ultimately through Jesus). I believe that the evidence for the inspiration and authority of the Bible is overwhelming, and I would be foolish in the extreme to ignore the Bible's teaching or attempt to modify it because I think that I know better.

God has spoken. Are you willing to listen?

PERSONAL REFLECTION

Have you started to disregard some teachings of the Bible because they seem outdated? When there is a conflict between what God's Word says and what the world says, which do you listen to and which do you dismiss? Have you gradually developed a diminished view of the Bible's inspiration and authority?

God is calling you to trust and obey His Word, rather than the fallible teachings of mankind. Choose today whom you will serve.

GROUP DISCUSSION QUESTIONS

1. Share your thoughts and impressions from this chapter. What was new to you? What was helpful? Is there anything you are still unsure about?

Read 1 Thessalonians 2:13

2. Although the words of scripture were written and spoken by people, what does this verse reveal about the true nature of these writings?

3. What does the last part of the verse mean when it refers to "the Word of God, which is indeed at work in you who believe"? In what way is it "at work" within us?

Read Hebrews 4:12

4. What does this tell us about the power and efficacy of God's Word? What does it do?

Read 2 Timothy 3:14-17

5. What does verse 15 tell us about what Holy Scripture can do? What does this say about churches and individuals who adopt evangelism strategies that have very little to do with the scriptures?

6. Verse 16 describes are the four distinct functions that the scriptures fulfill in the life of a Christian. What are they? Explain the distinct differences between each of the four.

7. Verse 17 describes the practical result of the fourth function in the previous verse. Explain the link.

Read Isaiah 55:8-11

8. This is a beautiful passage that describes the transcendent mind of God and the eternal purposes that he will inevitably accomplish through His Word. What important concept do verses 8-9 explain? What practical applications might this have for us as we go about our daily lives? How might this understanding change our response to some circumstances?

9. The rain and snow that water and nourish the Earth (in verse 10) is compared to the Word of God (in verse 11). Explain the parallels that are implicit in this comparison. How are they alike?

10. Notice the description of the origin of God's word in the beginning of verse 11. In what sense does it "go out from my [God's] mouth"? How should this impact our view of the Bible?

11. What is the "purpose" of God's Word, that is referred to but not described in verse 11? What is your understanding of its purpose?

11

BE COMMITTED TO READING GOD'S WORD

To this point we have examined the evidence for the Bible's authority and trustworthiness. We have seen compelling evidence that it is textually reliable, historically accurate, divinely inspired and personally transformative. If this is all true (and it is) then, surely, the Bible is a book worth reading!

The Apostle Paul, writing to the young pastor, Timothy, urges him to *devote* himself to reading the scriptures, and points him to their significant value:

> "All scripture is God-breathed and is useful for teaching, rebuking, correcting and training in righteousness, so that the person of God may be thoroughly equipped for every good work." (2 Timothy 3:16-17).

This is a helpful verse for summarising why we ought to read the Bible for ourselves.

Firstly, reading the Bible is worthwhile because it is a message from God himself. 2 Timothy 3:16 declares that the Bible is

"God-breathed". The Greek word used at this point is *"theopneustos" (θεοπνευστος)*, which literally means *"breathed out or exhaled by God"*. The Bible is not merely a collection of random thoughts from human authors. It is a message from our Creator, carefully crafted and meticulously preserved over millennia. It is a message from God to mankind, telling us how we can know him and receive a place in his eternal kingdom. Our Creator has written us a letter, and this ought to be of interest to every person on the planet! If that's not enough incentive to read a book, I don't know what is!

Secondly, apart from the compelling nature of its ultimate authorship, the Bible also commends itself to us because of what reading it will do for us. Notice that 2 Timothy 3:16 declares that reading the Bible will do four things for us: teach, rebuke, correct and train us in righteousness:

- *"Teaching"* – In a world where the concept of truth is becoming increasingly fuzzy and subjective, the Bible offers us God's unchanging truth. It declares God's truth about human nature, about our ultimate purpose, about right and wrong, about the nature and character of God himself, about salvation, about how we can continue to live in a right relationship with God, and about our eternal destiny. That is truth that is worth discovering! For those of us who have been Christians for many years, we will never reach a point where we don't need to be reminded of these truths and explore them more deeply. Reading the Bible regularly will keep these truths sharp and clear in our mind, in a world that is drifting further and further from God's truth.

- *"Rebuking"* – As fallen human beings, we will sometimes sin. But if we are regularly reading the Bible, it has a way of confronting us with our sin and convicting us of our wrongdoing. It will confront us with our wrong attitudes and selfish actions. As we read God's message, the Holy Spirit will convict our hearts and bring to our attention those things that God wants us to deal with.

- *"Correcting"* – The Bible doesn't just make us feel guilty about our wrong attitudes or actions. It points us on the path to correction and restitution. It tells us what we must do to get back on God's path when we have started to stray from it. It guides us in confessing our sins and turning from them, and outlines practical steps towards restitution and reconciliation where appropriate.

- *"Training in righteousness, so that the person of God may be thoroughly equipped for every good work"* – Christians are called to two important tasks: to grow more Christ-like and to serve in God's kingdom. The Bible provides inspiration and practical training in both these areas: *"training in righteousness"* (personal holiness) and *"equipped for every good work"* (practical service for God).

Paul's second letter to Timothy is not the only scripture passage that highlights the advantages of reading God's Word. There are many others. The opening verses of the first Psalm of the Bible provide a beautiful, poetic description of the benefits of regularly reading God's Word:

> "Blessed is the one who does not walk in step with the wicked or stand in the way that sinners take or sit in the company of mockers, but whose delight is in the law of the Lord, and who meditates on his law day and night. That person is like a tree planted by streams of water, which yields its fruit in season and whose leaf does not wither— whatever they do prospers." (Psalm 1:1-3)

In particular, notice the implied exhortation to meditate on God's Word "day and night". This is not advocating some kind of navel-gazing Eastern mysticism, but rather, a daily, penetrating contemplation of the application of the Bible's teaching to our lives. Notice, too, the Psalm's description of the benefits of this kind of regular contemplative Bible reading. The person who does this will be like a tree that is strong and fruitful because that person is continually drawing on the life-giving sustenance of God's Word.

Psalm 19 provides another beautiful poetic description of the benefits of regular Bible reading:

> "The law of the Lord is perfect, refreshing the soul. The statutes of the Lord are trustworthy, making wise the simple. The precepts of the Lord are right, giving joy to the heart. The commands of the Lord are radiant, giving light to the eyes." (Psalm 19:7-8)

Notice the four clear benefits of Bible reading that are mentioned in this psalm: refreshment, wisdom, joy and guidance. Who doesn't need these things? Who doesn't *want* these things?

Given the many and clear benefits that reading God's Word provides us with, one would expect that every Christian would be reading their Bible every day. Sadly, that is not the case. Many Christians rarely open their Bible from one week to the next. Several long-term sociological surveys of church attenders over many decades have revealed that personal Bible reading has significantly declined in recent years. There are several probable factors that have contributed to this decline. Two are worth briefly mentioning. Firstly, the rise of post-modernism and its associated loss of belief in absolute truth has resulted in a decline in belief in the Bible's authority, even among church people. Secondly, the rise of the internet, including streaming services and social media, has created an entertainment explosion. As a result of this, three disturbing trends have resulted:

1. Many people are now addicted to online entertainment and social media, which consumes vast amounts of their time.
2. Compared to the visually stimulating online world, reading the Bible now seems mundane and boring to many people.
3. The constant stimulation of visual media has led to a documented decrease in attention span and diminished literacy rates. Consequently, reading a book – even the Bible – is much more of a 'chore' than it used to be.

What should our response be?

I encourage you to examine your own life to see if daily Bible-reading has dropped off the bottom of your 'to do' list. If it has, I urge you to make a fresh commitment to spend time each day reading God's personal letter to you.

In the rest of this chapter I want to provide you with some practical tips on how to make Bible reading a daily habit that you come to love.

PRACTICAL TIPS FOR DAILY BIBLE READING

MAKE A REGULAR TIME AND PLACE

This might sound completely obvious, but if you don't establish a set routine, if you simply decide to *'get around to it when it's convenient'* each day, you will probably never get around to it. Having a set time each day for reading the Bible is far more likely to result in you *actually reading the Bible*. I have a morning routine that I follow most days, which is very simple and easy. Firstly, I get up and go for a run. When I return home, I make a bowl of muesli and I read the Bible while I eat breakfast at the kitchen bench. Following that, I pray. This works for me because we no longer have children living at home who need to be fed and made ready for school. It is a peaceful, quiet time where I can focus on God's Word and let him speak to me by his Spirit.

I can't predict what the best time and place for you is. But I can predict that if you don't set a definite time and place, you will almost certainly not be successful in developing a daily Bible reading habit.

START SMALL

If you start by setting yourself the unrealistic goal of reading 10 chapters of the Bible each day, your chance of still being engaged in daily Bible reading after a month is pretty slim! Why not start by reading a single chapter each day? The average Bible chapter has about 26 verses, which should take you about three minutes if you are a slow reader. Then you can spend another two minutes contemplating what you have just read and asking God to show you what he wants you to learn from it.

Just five minutes a day is not too much to ask, is it? And the fact that it is only five minutes means that it will not loom as large in your mind or seem as daunting a task as if it is a ten-chapter daily marathon that you have set yourself. You are much more likely to read your Bible, even on a very busy day, if you know that it will only take five minutes.

Of course, it is my hope that your daily Bible reading will become so helpful and rewarding for you, that it will eventually blossom into a more protracted time. But the key to starting well and staying the course is to start small at first.

PRAY FOR A RENEWED HEART

If you currently have little or no passion for Bible reading, the first step is to ask God to change your heart. Ask him to give you a desire to read his Word. But don't sit around waiting for the desire to take hold of you before you start reading. Reading the Bible will, itself, increase your desire to read the Bible! As you read God's Word each day, it will begin to change your heart. It will inspire you. It will strengthen your faith. It will fill you with hope and remind you of your purpose. You will gradually develop a taste for God's Word – a spiritual hunger for it – as you see its benefits begin to unfold in your life. But especially in the early stages, asking God to place a desire for His Word in your heart is a very helpful thing to do.

READ EVERYTHING IN CONTEXT

Context is King! No verse of the Bible exists as an isolated, independent precept. Each verse must be read in the context of its immediate passage, the theme and flow of the whole book, its literary genre, its place in covenantal history, its cultural context, its lexical context, and the context of any specific historical precipitating events that might have given rise to a particular statement. Taking all these contextual factors into account, however, can be quite complex, requiring a comprehensive understanding of the Bible and its cultural and historical background. It is a daunting task for the ordinary Bible reader who is not a biblical scholar. This pre-empts my next tip.

USE A RELIABLE STUDY BIBLE

A Study Bible is an extremely tool for any Bible reader. For the average person who does not wish to spend a fortune on Bible commentaries, a Study Bible is an inexpensive tool that provides essential insights from some of the world's most respected Bible scholars. In particular, a Study Bible provides:

- **Introductions** to books of the Bible, including the purpose, occasion and theme of the book, any precipitating historical events, as well as any other distinctive characteristics.
- **Explanatory footnotes.** While these are not as comprehensive as a dedicated Bible commentary, they provide a succinct explanation of the meaning of key verses and they outline any relevant cultural or historical context.
- **Textual footnotes.** These will indicate the presence of any textual variants that may have an impact on the meaning of the text.
- **Cross referencing.** This allows you to easily check other textual locations where the same theme or topic is addressed. The importance of checking cross-referencing cannot be over-estimated, as other Bible passages will often have a moderating influence on the interpretation of the verse or passage you are considering, and will allow you to build a comprehensive and balanced understanding of the topic.

- **Maps and timelines.** These occasional visual aids can be a valuable tool in providing context and overview.

USE A BIBLE APP

I can't recommend this highly enough. A decent Bible app on your computer or other device will open up a whole new world of resources to help you understand the Bible and get the most from your Bible reading. These include:

- Multiple translations to compare alternate readings. Most apps will allow you to have multiple translations open simultaneously.
- Greek / Hebrew meanings of words. In most apps, simply by highlighting a word in the Bible text, a secondary window will open, providing you with the original Greek or Hebrew word, together with its concise dictionary definition and a link to other passages where the same word is used.
- A range of free online commentaries (usually quite old but still helpful). These can provide valuable assistance in explaining difficult passages.
- Contemporary Bible commentaries that can be purchased through the app, at a fraction of their hard copy price.
- A search and cross-referencing system that enables you to quickly jump to other similar passages with the touch of a finger or the click of a mouse.

A Bible app is a convenient means of tapping into a world of scholarly resources. Some apps are free, but the better ones will require a small expenditure. In my opinion, it is the best money you will ever spend! I happen to use the Olive Tree Bible App, but there are plenty of other very good apps out there.

READ THE WHOLE BIBLE

There is no better way of developing a contextual understanding of biblical truth than reading the whole book. I am surprised at how many Christians have never actually read the whole Bible. They may have read dozens of novels, read hundreds of blogs, listened to hundreds of podcasts, watched hundreds of movies and listened to hundreds of musical albums, but they have never bothered to read the whole of God's Word at least once in their life. One of the reasons for this is that it seems a daunting task. After all, the Bible is a big book. But if it is broken down into daily portions, it is very achievable.

When I was a Biblical Studies teacher, I used to do an interesting class activity. I got all the students to read a single chapter of the Bible, and each student timed how long it took them, reading at a comfortable pace. The average time was 2 minutes 30 seconds. I rounded that up to 3 minutes to be generous. I then explained to the class that the Bible contains 1,189 chapters. We calculated that reading the whole Bible would take 3,567 minutes (1,189 chapters x 3 minutes). Therefore, to read the whole Bible in one year would take 3,567 minutes divided by 365 days, which turns out to be just 9.7 minutes per day.

In other words, just 10 minutes per day would enable you to read the entire Bible in one year. Most people spend much more than 10 minutes each day on social media or watching TV. How important is God's Word to you? The more you read it, and the more familiar you become with the flow of its story, the better you will be able to interpret its message contextually.

Alternatively, you may decide to only read through the New Testament in one year. This is an even more achievable goal. The New Testament contains 260 chapters. Using the same calculations as the one for the whole Bible, it will take you only two minutes each day to read through the New Testament in one year! This does not seem too great a commitment, considering how much time we spend each day absorbing frivolous entertainment.

READ PRAYERFULLY

In the end, the Bible is a spiritual book that requires spiritual insight. It is the Holy Spirit who brings the words of this book to life, enlightening our minds, convicting our hearts and inspiring our spirits. Without the Spirit's illuminating work within us, the Bible is simply a collection of words. We need to read the Bible with a prayerful heart, trusting in the Holy Spirit to open our hearts and minds to God's message so that we can correctly discern and apply God's truth to our lives. All the hermeneutical principles and Bible commentaries in the world cannot do this. We need the Holy Spirit to breathe life into the words that we read, so that their message penetrates our hearts and transforms us from within. For this reason, it is very helpful to ask the Holy Spirit to illuminate our understanding as we read and reflect on the meaning and application of a Bible passage.

JOIN A BIBLE STUDY GROUP

The insight and perspective of other Christians can be extremely helpful in broadening your own understanding. Christians aren't meant to fly solo. We need each other. The wisdom of God's Spirit is more clearly manifest when we meet together than when we sit at home trying to read the Bible on our own. This is why the writer to Hebrews exhorts us, *"Do not give up meeting together, as some are in the habit of doing"* (Heb 10:25). Often the meaning of a passage that is obscure to you will become much clearer when others contribute their insights. Why not consider joining a Bible study group for just one term and see how it goes? If you are already a member of a Bible Study group, is there a friend you could invite who would benefit from being part of your group as well?

CONCLUSION

It is my hope and prayer that your trust in the Bible is firmer, your faith in its inspiration is clearer, and your commitment to reading it is much stronger.

Charles Spurgeon, the great preacher of the 19th century, once commented,

"Why is it that some Christians, although they hear many sermons, make such slow advances in the divine life? Because they neglect their [prayer] closets, and do not thoughtfully meditate on God's Word. They love the wheat, but they do not grind it; they would have the corn, but they will not go forth into the fields to gather it; the fruit hangs upon the tree, but they will not pluck it; the water flows at their feet, but they will not stoop to drink it. From such folly deliver us, O Lord."

It is my hope and prayer that you will make a fresh commitment to reading God's Word and, in so doing, find the refreshment, wisdom, joy and guidance that the psalmist wrote about so long ago:

"The law of the Lord is perfect, refreshing the soul. The statutes of the Lord are trustworthy, making wise the simple. The precepts of the Lord are right, giving joy to the heart. The commands of the Lord are radiant, giving light to the eyes." (Psalm 19:7-8)

PERSONAL REFLECTION

Do you sense God's Spirit calling you to recommit yourself to reading God's Word? Make a decision, right now, to start reading the Bible regularly. Decide a place and time when you can do this without interruption. Get that Bible down off the shelf and dust it off!

Perhaps you could consider buying a Bible-reading aid? What about a Bible app or a new Study Bible? Spending a few dollars to set yourself up can reinforce your commitment to make a new start and can inject a degree of enthusiasm into your renewed spiritual resolution.

If you are still struggling to be motivated, be honest with God about it. Pray and ask him to inspire you and give you a desire to read his Word.

GROUP DISCUSSION QUESTIONS

1. Share your thoughts and impressions from this chapter. What was new to you? What was helpful? Is there anything you are still unsure about?

Read Psalm 1:1-3

2. What is verse 1 calling us to do (or not do)?

3. What does it mean to "delight" in God's Word (verse 2)?

4. Verse 2 also calls us to "meditate on his law, day and night". This is not referring to some kind of esoteric mystical meditation, but a very simple, practical approach to reading the Bible. Explain what it means to "meditate" on God's Word.

5. Verse 3 describes some of the blessings that will inevitably flow from immersing ourselves in God's Word. What are they?

Read Psalm 19:7-8

6. These two verses describe God's Word as "perfect ... trustworthy ... right ... radiant". They also describe four distinct things that God's Word can do for us if we read it. What are those four things? Explain each of them in different words.

Read Deuteronomy 11:18-21

After God rescued the Israelites from slavery in Egypt, he made a new covenant with them, through Moses. As part of his instructions for them he gave these strong exhortations regarding their need to memorise His Word. Speaking of the commandments and instructions God had given through Moses, God now instructed his people to memorise them and teach them to each successive generation.

7. What do you think each of the following phrases symbolises:

- "tie them as symbols on your hands" (verse 18). (In other words, why the hands?)

- "bind them on your foreheads" (Why their foreheads?)

- "Write them on the doorframes of your houses and on your gates" (Why their doors and gates?)

8. In what ways should this symbolism have parallels for us today?

9. Read verse 19. What is this asking us to do?

10. Read verse 21. What kind of blessing does this infer will result from doing this?

Read James 1:22-25

11. This passage is a New testament parallel with the previous passage from Deuteronomy. Identify the parallels and discuss their practical applications for us today.

12. One of the ways of not 'forgetting' what God's Word says, is to actually memorise Bible verses. Have any of you ever done this? How helpful has it been? Is there a method of memorisation that you have tried that works?

∽

PART IV

CONNECTING WITH GOD'S FAMILY

12

LOVE ME, LOVE MY FAMILY

Over the years I have encountered many people who have become estranged from members of their own immediate family: siblings who haven't spoken for decades and children who have left home and refuse to have any contact with their parents. Family disassociation is a surprisingly common scenario. Almost always it arises from hurtful experiences a person may have had with members of their family. They have been treated badly, misunderstood, not loved, neglected, ridiculed, abused, left out of wills, ripped off, victimised ... The list goes on and on. And so the person who perceives themselves to be the victim turns their back and walks away. They leave their family. They disown them and cut off all ties with the people who have hurt them and let them down.

Tragically, this same scenario can sometimes play out in the family of God. There are many people who were once active members of the Christian church but who are now completely estranged from God's family. They have walked away, shaking the dust from their feet, because of their perception of having been treated badly. They were not loved and supported as they feel they should have been. Or perhaps they were the victims of gossip or slander. Others leave because they become disillusioned when they see some kind of ungodly behaviour or hypocrisy among the church leaders, or because they become disheartened by the power-plays and politics of church life.

Yes, there are many ex-church members out there. Maybe you are one, yourself. Maybe you are still licking your wounds after being treated badly by brothers and sisters in Christ who should know better. Maybe you became so disillusioned by the unhealthy way the church operated that you felt you could no longer be part of it. Or perhaps you merely felt completely ignored and neglected – an irrelevant church attender whose eventual departure was not even noted or responded to.

So, now you are 'flying solo'. You still believe in God. You still acknowledge Christ as your Lord and Saviour. But you won't set foot inside a church again. Or perhaps you have become a spiritual drifter. Occasionally sticking your nose inside a church, but never putting down any spiritual roots in any one congregation. Never opening yourself to being committed to a group of people who might let you down again. Refusing to become an integral part of an organisation which you now perceive to be deeply flawed. The institutional church has failed to live up to your high expectations, and you no longer wish to be an active part of it.

Is that you? Have I just described your situation? If I have, I hope and pray that you will read this chapter with an open heart and mind, because God does not want you to stay as you are. In fact, God grieves over your current attitude to his family.

In order to understand how important it is for a Christian to belong to a church, it is helpful to examine the key metaphors that the Bible uses to describe the church.

THE CHURCH AS GOD'S FAMILY

The Bible repeatedly describes the church as God's family. For example:

> "For this reason I bow my knees to the Father of our Lord Jesus Christ, from whom the whole <u>family</u> in heaven and earth is named" (Ephesians 3:14, 15)

Furthermore, we are not just distant relatives; we are God's *immediate* family, living in his household:

> "Now, therefore, you are no longer strangers and foreigners, but fellow citizens with the saints and of the <u>household of God</u>, and have been built on the foundation of the apostles and prophets, Jesus Christ Himself being the chief cornerstone." (Ephesians 2:19)

Suppose you came to me and said, "I really like you and I want to be your friend, but I want nothing to do with your family. I don't like your wife, I hate your daughter and I can't stand your son. I want nothing to do with them, but let's be friends." How do you think I would respond? Do you think I would enthusiastically embrace you as my friend? If you think this attitude of disengagement and dislike towards my family is a sound basis for a close friendship with me, you are deeply mistaken! At best, I might be willing to relate to you politely and superficially, but if you want nothing to do with my family, we could never truly become friends – at least not at any deep level.

This doesn't mean that I am under any illusions regarding my family. I am fully aware that they are not perfect. I see their faults and foibles. I am not blind to their imperfections. After all, I know them better than you do. But I love them anyway, despite their weaknesses and inconsistencies. And anyone wanting to form a close friendship with me, must also accept my family, just as they are.

How do you think God feels towards his family, the church on Earth? As much as I love my own family, God's love for his family is infinitely greater.

> *"For Christ loved the church and gave himself up for her"* (Ephesians 5:25).

God loves his family, the church, so much that he sacrificed his Son to redeem it. Those who think they can have a close connection with God but be completely disconnected from his family, fail to understand how deeply God loves his family and how important it is that you remain actively committed to it.

THE CHURCH AS CHRIST'S BRIDE

In Revelation 19:7, the church is described as the *"bride"* of Christ and Jesus is depicted as preparing a great feast to welcome his beloved bride into heaven. Ephesians 5:25-27 contains this same analogy of the church as Christ's bride, telling us that Christ loves his bride so much, that he sacrificed his life for her.

This is an extraordinary metaphor. That the church should be described as Christ's bride, speaks of a love that is passionate and profound. Indeed, passion is an entirely appropriate word to use for God's love towards his bride, provided we don't endow it with sexual connotations. On several occasions, the Bible even speaks of God as being "jealous" for his people, not wanting their affections to be turned from him towards false gods / husbands (Exodus 20:5-6; 34:14).

If you are married, can you remember the feeling of absolute love and adoration that you felt on the day you stood next to your betrothed and made your wedding vows together? Can you remember how besotted you were (and hopefully still are)? That is a small picture of how much God loves his church. Furthermore, can you imagine someone coming up to you immediately after your wedding ceremony, as you mingled with your wedding guests, and saying to you, *"I love you, but I can't stand your wife / husband"*? It would be unthinkable, wouldn't it? Yet this is what some people are effectively saying to God. How do you imagine God feels about this?

THE CHURCH AS CHRIST'S BODY

The image of the church as the body of Christ is another foundational biblical metaphor. In fact, this is the most common analogy, used over forty times in the New Testament. Here are just a couple of instances:

> *"Now you are Christ's body, and individual members of it"* (1 Corinthians 12:27)

> *"We, who are many, are one body in Christ, and individually members one of another."* (Romans 12:5)

In these verses, notice the acknowledgment of both our individuality AND our connectedness to one another. Indeed, there is a strong inference in the New Testament that it is only when we are in connection with each other that the body is healthy and we, as individual parts of the body, are also healthy.

This analogy of the church being like a physical body is an important one, and we need to follow the analogy through to its logical conclusion. In regard to our physical body, if we start hacking off parts of our body and discarding them, (or if some parts of my body abandon me of their own accord!), the parts that are separated from me will die and I, as a whole body, will become impaired.

What is true of the physical body is also true spiritually. Christians who decide to turn their back on the body of Christ and fly solo inevitably end up weaker and almost always drift into moral failure or theological error. They are more easily led into temptation, more prone to sin, less inclined to read their Bible, less inclined to pray and often end up falling away altogether. They die spiritually – slowly and incrementally. For a time, they may continue to adhere to the central truths of the Christian faith and abide by its values. But, as time passes, the loss of Christian fellowship with its associated encouragement, mutual edification and personal accountability, results in the fire of a person's faith slowly fading until it is eventually extinguished – swamped by the more insistent values and beliefs of the world. I have seen this happen time and time again.

Our need to remain connected to Christ's body, the church, is nowhere more clearly explained than in Ephesians. In chapter 4, he explains that it is only by being united in fellowship with a body of believers that we can reach maturity in Christ. He pleads with us to:

> "*13 ... all reach unity in the faith ... 14 Then we will no longer be infants, tossed back and forth by the waves, and blown here and there by every wind of teaching and by the cunning and craftiness of people in their deceitful scheming. 15 Instead, speaking the truth in love, we will grow to become in every respect the mature body of him who is the head, that is, Christ. 16 From him the whole body, joined and held together by every supporting ligament, grows and builds itself up in love, as each part does its work."* (Ephesians 4:14-16)

It is only by remaining connected in close fellowship with other Christians that we can protect ourselves from being *"tossed back and forth by the waves, and blown here and there by every wind of teaching and by the cunning and craftiness of people in their deceitful scheming" (verse 15)*. It is the mutual accountability and regular encouragement of other believers *"speaking the truth in love"* that will continue to guide and protect us so that *"we will grow to become in every respect the mature body of him who is the head, that is, Christ"* (verse 15). And it is only by the use of our complementary gifts, as we serve God together, that we can exercise a balanced ministry and experience the fullness of Christ's gifts as He works among us:

> *"From him the whole body, joined and held together by every supporting ligament, grows and builds itself up in love, as each part does its work."* (verse 16)

Paul's choice of the word 'ligaments' in this verse is significant. Ligaments are extremely tough, fibrous bonds that are very difficult to break. This is the kind of strong connection that God intends for Christians to have with each other. We aren't designed to fly solo. We are meant to be connected with each other.

CHRIST, THE HEAD OF THE BODY

Did you notice the reference to Christ as the head of his body, in Ephesians 4:15? Paul repeats this metaphor in his letter to the Colossians:

> *"And he [Christ] is the head of the body, the church."* (Colossians 1:18)

I want you to think about this analogy very carefully. Have you ever seen a head connected to only a hand? Have you ever seen a head with no body at all, but with just a single small bodily part attached to it? Of course not. Yet this is how solo Christians see themselves. They believe they can be connected to Christ individually, without belonging to a body of believers. But logically and biblically, this cannot be. A foot or hand is only connected to the head by remaining a part of the whole body. A bodily part that removes itself from the body, also loses its connection to the head and dies. The same is true spiritually.

The essential nature of being connected to Christ's body is evident in a statement that Paul makes, in 1 Corinthians 12, which is quite astounding:

> *"Just as a body, though one, has many parts, but all its many parts form one body, so it is with Christ. For we were all baptized by one Spirit into one body." (1 Corinthians 12:13)*

Paul is saying that when you became a Christian, when you were *"baptised by one Spirit"* (the moment when the Holy Spirit came to reside within you at the moment of your conversion), you were joined not only to Christ himself, but were bound, spiritually, to his church on Earth. You were baptised into the church, Christ's body, and it is your incorporation into his church that connects you to Christ as its head.

We must be careful not to push this theology too far. Church membership is not the means of salvation. A personal response to Christ as Saviour and Lord is what is needed. A person is not saved because they have joined the church. It is the other way around: a person has joined the church because they have been saved. But the point is, membership of the church on Earth is the inextricable, inescapable result of your salvation. You cannot avoid it.

Yet there are those who *do* try to avoid it.

A MODERN PLAGUE

The rise of 'solo Christianity' is a relatively recent phenomena, fuelled by the rise of the philosophy of individualism that now pervades our society generally. *"It's all about me"* is the mantra of the modern world, and this attitude has subtly influenced many people of faith. They see no problem in rejecting the church and flying solo. This is because they have no sense of allegiance to anything beyond their own needs and wants.

The *'I love Jesus but can't stand the church'* narrative is unfortunately all too common within modern Christian culture. A new anti-church brand of Christianity has arisen, partly fuelled by social distancing in response to recent pandemics, which has led a growing number of Christians to walk away from a commitment to a local community of believers and adopt a solo brand of Christianity. Some of these solo Christians are the walking-wounded – those who have been hurt or disillusioned by the church's imperfections and have turned their backs on it, nursing their bitterness. Others simply see no great need to be part of a Christian community. The world-wide web now allows them to practice a kind of 'smorgasbord Christianity', where they graze on sermons and worship services from all over the world, taking what they want, without needing to give back. They are not part of a functioning, interconnected body, but are mere isolated entities, adrift and unconnected, grazing at will on whatever spiritual pastures suit them from day to day.

In the midst of his discourse on the church as the body of Christ, Paul writes:

> "The eye cannot say to the hand, 'I don't need you!'. And the hand cannot say to the feet, 'I don't need you!'" (1 Corinthians 12:21)

Yet this is exactly what solo Christians are effectively saying. They believe they don't need the church and think that their spiritual isolation is acceptable to God.

The argument that I have heard from solo Christians is that they don't need to attend a physical meeting of Christians in a physical location to be part of Christ's body. They argue that the body of Christ is his spiritual body comprised of every person who accepts Christ as Lord and Saviour, irrespective of whether they are committed to a local church gathering. But this view fails to appreciate the clear scriptural link between membership of Christ's spiritual body and membership of a physical body of believers.

This strong link is evident in Paul's first letter to the Corinthians when he addresses the case of a man in the church who is openly practising incest. Because the man is unrepentant, Paul commands the church to excommunicate him, to cast him out from their physical fellowship. Paul explains that this act of excommunication will effectively *"hand this man over to Satan for the destruction of his flesh"* (1 Corinthians 5:5). This is an incredibly strong statement! According to this Bible passage, cutting a person off from a physical body of believers results in that person also being cut off from the spiritual body of Christ! The person is effectively removed from the saving headship of Christ by being amputated from his physical body on Earth. (It is worth pointing out that this severe act of excommunication at Corinth was done with the aim of bringing about the man's repentance and his eventual restoration to Christ and his church, which is, indeed, what eventually happened – 2 Corinthians 2:4-16).

THE NEED FOR A FAMILY REUNION

The modern plague of anti-church, solo Christianity fails to appreciate how it grieves God's heart when a person walks away from God's family, rejects his beloved bride and amputates themselves from his body on Earth. God loves his church, despite its faults and weaknesses. Christ died for his beloved bride, even though he sees its blemishes more clearly than you or I do. It may, at times, be a deeply dysfunctional family, but it is God's dearly beloved family, and he asks us not to walk away from it.

Are you an estranged family member? Or, if not completely estranged, are you an aloof family member? Perhaps you have not completely walked away. You may still be loosely connected, but that connection has been weakened over the years because of the hurts or disillusionment that you have experienced. You keep God's family at a distance now. You may still turn up to church, but you are no longer as committed as you once were. You've removed yourself from the various serving rosters and stepped down from ministries that you were once so committed to. You're still in the boat, but you are no longer pulling on an oar alongside your brothers and sisters. You are still present at gatherings, but emotionally distant, no longer trusting yourself to the family that has disappointed you so badly in the past.

I know how you feel. I am not judging you. Because I have been there too. I have walked in your shoes. There was a time in my life when I experienced some profound disappointments with a church I was involved with. My family and I eventually moved to a new city and a new church, but despite the fact that the new church had nothing to do with the hurts we had experienced in the past, for years afterwards I kept myself at a distance from my brothers and sisters in Christ. I found it hard to trust again. I found it hard to be committed and to be enthusiastic. Even now, though I have completely forgiven those who wounded me in the past and I no longer feel any hurt or anger or bitterness, I am more guarded in my relationships than I used to be.

But I am absolutely convinced of my need to be an active part of God's family. I cannot be connected to the Head without being connected to his body as well.

What about you? Is God calling you to reconnect with his body? Is he calling you to come back to his family? Is he challenging you to leave your past hurts and disappointments behind and fully re-engage with his people?

The writer to the Hebrews exhorts us:

> *"Let us consider how we may spur one another on toward love and good deeds, not giving up meeting together, as some are in the habit of doing, but encouraging one another – and all the more as you see the Day approaching." (Hebrews 10:24-25)*

This is a Bible passage for our times, because there are, indeed, many today who are *"in the habit of"* giving up meeting together. This passage is a rallying call for today's Christians! In a society which now prizes individualism, we are exhorted; *"let us not give up meeting together."* Though many seek to be solo Christians; *"let us not give up meeting together."* Furthermore, we are called to not merely turn up at church gatherings – to be physically present but relatively unconnected and uncommitted. No. This verse is demanding much more from us. It calls us into a deep connection with our brothers and sisters in Christ. We are to *"consider how we may spur one another on toward love and good deeds"*. We are exhorted to *"encourage one another – and all the more as you see the Day approaching."* This is not describing mere disconnected church attendance. God is calling us to be fully committed to his family, just as he is. We are called to serve alongside our brothers and sisters and be fully committed to their welfare and spiritual growth.

Are you seeking a deeper, stronger connection with God? I can guarantee you will never find that connection as a solo Christian, disconnected from his body. Despite all its faults and weaknesses, the church on Earth remains the vessel in which, and through which, God most clearly chooses to manifest himself to the world today:

> *"And in him you too are being built together to become a dwelling in which God lives by his Spirit."* (Ephesians 2:22)

Although God's Spirit lives within each of us, individually, there is a special sense in which the presence of God resides within his people when they meet together corporately. When we come together in deep fellowship, we become *"a dwelling in which God lives by his Spirit."* (Ephesians 2:22). Jesus referred to this enhanced or focused presence of God in corporate gatherings when he said, *"Whenever two or three gather in my name, there I am in their midst"* (Matthew 18:20). This does not infer that Christ is not present with us when we are alone, for God is omnipresent – with us everywhere, all the time. But there is a sense in which Christ's presence is made more tangible, more obvious to our senses, more evident to our minds and hearts, through the mutual ministry of Christians when we meet together to share our faith and to worship God. In the warmth of Christian fellowship, God's presence is more tangibly obvious and our faith is strengthened.

So, don't stay out there in the cold, all alone. Come in and join us!

PERSONAL REFLECTION

Have you been hurt or disappointed by the church in the past? Do you still carry unforgiveness in your heart towards those who let you down? If so, you need to spend some time in prayer, asking for the Holy Spirit to enable you to forgive them and to finally release the burden of hurt and bitterness that you have been carrying around.

Have you distanced yourself from the body of Christ? Have you left it altogether? Or perhaps you have been physically present but emotionally distant and spiritually uncommitted. Spend some time now asking God to help you to commit yourself afresh to a deeper fellowship with the family of God.

GROUP DISCUSSION QUESTIONS

1. Share your thoughts and impressions from this chapter. What was new to you? What was helpful? Is there anything you are still unsure about?

Read Ephesians 2:19-22

2. In the chapter you have just read, we examined three biblical metaphors for the church: the family of God, the bride of Christ and the body of Christ. In this passage we find a reference to one of those, plus a fourth metaphor that we did not have time or space to discuss in this chapter. Firstly, when verse 19 describes Christians as *"members of his household"*, what kinds of images come to mind for you? What does this metaphor teach us about our relationship to God and to each other?

3. Verses 20-22 introduce a fourth metaphor for the church. What is it? What does this teach us about our relationship to each other as Christians? See what aspects you can draw out of this analogy.

Read 1 Corinthians 12:12-31

4. Get each person in the group to share a brief thought about what most impacts them from this passage.

5. What does this passage tell us about why we need to be connected to each other as Christians?

6. Contrary to what some churches teach, the phrase *"baptised by one Spirit"* in verse13, does not refer to some kind of post-conversion experience of the Holy Spirit where a person starts speaking in tongues. This is clear from comparing this verse (*"For we were ALL baptised by one Spirit"*) to verse 30 (*"Do all speak in tongues?"*). In the Greek, this latter question is written in a very specific grammatical form with an implied *"No"*. Thus, to a church where not everyone speaks in tongues, Paul, nonetheless, states that they were ALL baptised by the Spirit. A more detailed study of the use of this term in the New Testament shows, very clearly, that it is always used of a person's initial reception of the Holy Spirit at conversion, and not of some post-conversion experience. What is more pertinent to our current discussion, however, is the result of this spiritual baptism. What are we baptised into? And what does this say about those who seek to live a solo Christian life?

Read Ephesians 4:11-16

7. There is absolutely no hint in this passage of the possibility of Christians "going it solo". What 'people resources' has God made available in the church to equip the whole body?

8. Read verse 12. What is the role of these ministry people? (Notice, please, that their primary role is not to run around doing all the ministry or "works of service" themselves!).

9. Read verses 13-14. How do you think being connected to the body of Christ, under godly leadership, provides us with protection?

10. Read verse 15. How does "speaking the truth in love" help Christians grow into maturity? What is meant by this?

11. Read verse 16. What does this teach us about our need to be part of local church?

Read Hebrews 10:24-25

12. In what ways can Christians *"spur one another on"*? Be specific.

13. What causes some people to give up meeting together? What can we do about this? How can we help those who have lost their connection to God's family?

14. What is the "Day" mentioned in verse 25 and why is it especially important to keep meeting together as that Day draws closer?

15. In your group prayer time, perhaps you could pray for people you know who have left the church for various reasons.

13

NO MAGIC PILL

We have now reached the end of our journey to seek a restored and revitalised connection with God. If you were not a Christian prior to this, I hope and pray that you have followed the steps in this book and are now beginning to explore a relationship with God that is enriching and transformative.

For readers who have been in the Christian faith for a while and are looking to revitalise your relationship with God, let me make a few final comments.

There is nothing particularly new in the things I have written. There is no new 'magic pill', no secret formula for renewal that you don't already know about. You probably already knew what you had to do before you read this book!

I think there is a tendency in all of us to look for the easy fix. Either that, or we look for some new, exotic or novel remedy that will instantly lift us out of our spiritual doldrums. In the mid-1990's, the 'Toronto Blessing' swept through the Christian world with an emphasis on being 'slain in the spirit' and on the strange phenomena of uncontrollable 'laughing in the Spirit'. It was the latest new 'thing' and many people – indeed, whole churches – lapped it up. But when the movement gradually faded away, what was noticeable was that those who had been caught up in it were no closer to God than before. In fact a very observable 'let down' often took place, which became known as 'Post Holy Laughter Depression Syndrome' (PHLDS).

Exotic quick fixes for spiritual malaise simply don't work. I could tell you to go and sit on top of a mountain for a month and eat sunflowers and grasshoppers but it would probably do you no good – except help you lose weight. The 'secret' to a vibrant, joyful walk with God is no secret at all. It really comes back to the basics, which you already know.

The 12 steps that I have outlined in this book, fall into four basic disciplines (which, you will notice, are the four sections of this book):

- Repentance

- Prayer

- Bible Reading

- Christian Fellowship and Mission

If your walk with God has become a little stale, if you are lacking the zeal and enthusiasm that you once experienced as a Christian, then I can guarantee that you have allowed at least one of these disciplines to slip.

There are books that propose a greater array of spiritual disciplines which involve other, more esoteric activities such as meditation, contemplation, fasting, solitude, simplicity and silence. I have tried all of these and found some value in them, but I keep coming back to the 'big four' that I have dealt with in this book. A Christian who is repenting daily (who has no habitual unconfessed sin in their life), who is praying and reading their Bible daily and is deeply committed to the fellowship and mission of their local church will experience the joy of a rich and fulfilling relationship with God. If your current walk with God seems stale and flat, you need to have a long hard look at each of these four areas to see what has slipped.

Although the key to a vibrant, joyful spiritual life is simple – just four key disciplines – that doesn't mean it is easy. It is simple, in the sense that it is uncomplicated. There is no mystical spiritual secret that you have to travel to India to discover, or spend months sitting on top of a mountain to work out. The path to spiritual renewal is the well-trodden path that you have known all along. But, as I said, that doesn't mean it is easy.

There is a reason why we call these things 'disciplines'. Because they take discipline! I do not always find my morning Bible reading and prayer time easy. Sometimes I jump out of bed and can't wait to read my Bible and pray, but other mornings I am less enthusiastic. This morning (before I wrote this chapter) was one of those latter mornings. I felt flat and tired. I could easily have skipped my 'quiet time' this morning. But I didn't. I forced myself to read the next couple of chapters of my Bible. I forced myself to pray. Because I know that I need to eat and breathe, spiritually, every day. The Bible is food for the soul and prayer is the breath of the soul, and I need these things every day of my life if I am to remain strong and healthy as a Christian.

If you sometimes struggle to be motivated to read your Bible and pray, you are not alone. If you sometimes feel like giving church a miss and just 'blobbing' at home, you are in good company. Even the great men and women of God have to battle similar spiritual inertia. In 1 Corinthians 9, Paul writes about his own need for self-discipline:

> "*[24] Do you not know that in a race all the runners run, but only one gets the prize? Run in such a way as to get the prize. [25] Everyone who competes in the games goes into strict training. They do it to get a crown that will not last, but we do it to get a crown that will last forever. [26] Therefore I do not run like someone running aimlessly; I do not fight like a boxer beating the air. [27] No, I strike a blow to my body and make it my slave so that after I have preached to others, I myself will not be disqualified for the prize.*" (1 Corinthians 9:24-27).

Notice the vigorous athletic imagery that Paul uses to describe his need for self-discipline. He likens himself to a boxer in a fight and a runner competing in a race, both of which require strict, even harsh, training. *"I strike a blow to my body"*, says Paul. It is a metaphor indicating the severity with which he disciplines himself to ensure that he successfully finishes the race of faith, so that he *"will not be disqualified for the prize."*

I would love to have included a sealed plastic pouch at the end of this book with a magic prayer or chant that could instantly transform your walk with God into a daily experience of joy and spiritual ecstasy. But no such quick fix exists. There are no short cuts. If you have become spiritually stale and are looking to reconnect with God in a deep way, you must discipline yourself to engage, daily, with the four key spiritual disciplines: repentance, prayer, Bible reading and Christian fellowship and mission. There is simply no other way.

There are two coffee shops with intriguing names that I have encountered over the years. One is called *The Daily Grind*. The other is called *The Happy Bean*. My daily quiet times are a lot like those two coffee shops. Some mornings I am a happy bean. I delight in praying and in reading God's Word. The morning's Bible passage inspires and challenges me, and I pray with great passion as the Holy Spirit moves me. Other mornings, my quiet time is more like a daily grind. Nothing really leaps out of the page at me and I work my way through my prayer list dutifully. On these mornings, I could easily give the whole thing a miss.

But I don't.

And here is where I really need you to pay attention.

The key to the establishment and maintenance of a vibrant spiritual life – of a joyful daily walk with God – is discipline. And discipline becomes most important on those 'daily grind' days. In fact, it is how we respond on those days that differentiates the strong Christian from the weak, the vibrant Christian from the stale. Because if you give in to your tiredness or lassitude on those 'daily grind' days, if you succumb to your laziness on those Sundays when you feel like blobbing at home, I can guarantee that you will have more and more 'daily grind' days, and less and less 'happy bean' days.

The main thing that differentiates the strong Christian from the weak, the vibrant Christian from the stale, is discipline. The strong Christian – the one who has a deep and vibrant connection with God – is the one who refuses to let the random fluctuations in their bio-rhythms dictate their spirituality. The strong Christian is the one who rises each day with a determination to meet with their Creator, irrespective of their mood swings and variable energy levels. They will not be put off. They *"strike a blow to [their] body"*. They beat into submission their natural laziness and spiritual disinclination. And they do this, because their eyes are fixed on a prize that is worth fighting for.

Having said all that, I want to stress that the disciplined spiritual life is not all drudgery and perfunctory duty. While it is true that there will always be 'daily grind' days, my experience is that the more regular and disciplined I am in having a daily time alone with God, the less 'daily grind' days there are. And even when a 'daily grind' day does come along, if I push through it, determined to meet with God anyway, I almost always emerge from that encounter enriched and thankful that I didn't give up.

It happened to me this morning. I started out in 'daily grind' mode, but, by the end, I emerged as a 'happy bean'.

Meeting with one's Creator will do that.

So, don't give up.

Don't give in.

Push on to the end, with discipline and determination, because you know that the ultimate prize is worth it.

> *"Therefore, since we are surrounded by such a great cloud of witnesses, let us throw off everything that hinders and the sin that so easily entangles. And let us run with perseverance the race marked out for us, fixing our eyes on Jesus, the pioneer and perfecter of our faith. For the joy set before him he endured the cross, scorning its shame, and sat down at the right hand of the throne of God. Consider him who endured such opposition from sinners, so that you will not grow weary and lose heart." (Hebrews 12:1-3)*

~

FREE SERMON OUTLINES

For preachers who want to link their sermons with their church's small group studies, below is a link to download FREE sermon outlines for each of the 12 topics. If you are reading this as an eBook, simply click or touch the link and follow the download directions. If you are reading the paperback version, simply type the link into your web browser.

SERMON OUTLINES can be downloaded from my Book-Funnel page, here:

https://dl.bookfunnel.com/oxtgpwsi89

ALSO BY KEVIN SIMINGTON

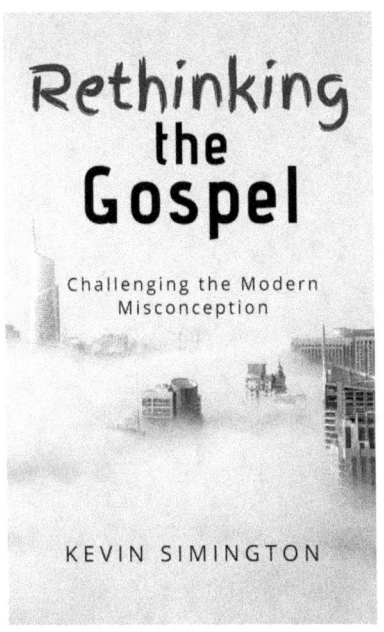

"*Rethinking the Gospel*" is a profoundly challenging exploration of the modern church's proclamation of the gospel. It examines an element of the gospel that has been largely ignored or under-emphasised since the start of the Reformation in the 1500's.

One reviewer commented: *"Every church pastor, preacher and Christian should read this book! It has transformed my understanding of the gospel."*

Another reviewer commented: *"This is a devastating and eye-opening commentary on the blight that has infiltrated the modern church. It is a wake-up call that desperately needs to be heard."*

"*Rethinking the Gospel*" is available in print or as an eBook from SmartFaith.net, Amazon and all major online retailers.

7 REASONS TO BELIEVE

"The clearest, most up-to-date defence of the existence of God and the truth of the Christian message that I have ever read!" (Review)

7 Reasons To Believe is a clear, powerful presentation of the seven most persuasive arguments for the existence of God. Compelling evidence is examined from the fields of microbiology, genetics, cosmology, history and personal experience. Peppered with wit and brimming with meticulously-researched facts, this book will challenge even the most hardened sceptics and will strengthen the faith of those who already believe.

7 Reasons to Believe is available from SmartFaith or Amazon.

FINDING GOD WHEN HE SEEMS TO BE HIDING

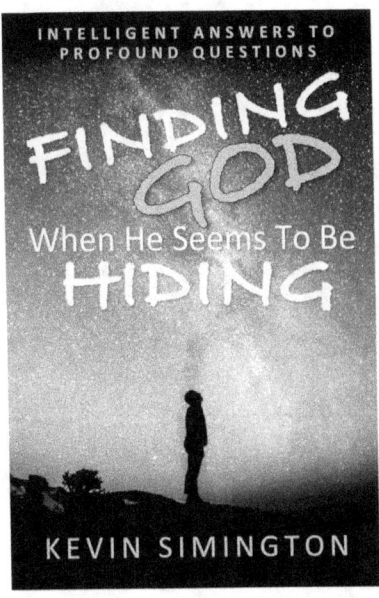

"*Finding God When He Seems to Be Hiding*" provides intelligent answers to the common questions and objections that are often roadblocks in people's journey towards faith. If God exists, why is there so much suffering in the world? What about all the killing in the Bible? How can a loving God send people to hell? Is the Bible reliable? What evidence is there for the resurrection of Jesus? What about evolution? Hasn't science and evolution disproved the existence of God? How can God permit abuse and religious violence?

This book addresses these and other common questions with remarkable clarity and provides answers that move beyond the standard, glib responses that are often proposed.

"*Finding God When He Seems To Be Hiding*" is available in print or as an eBook from SmartFaith.net, Amazon and all major online retailers.

MAKING SENSE OF THE BIBLE

This book will change the way you read the Bible!

"*Making Sense of the Bible*" is a comprehensive guide to understanding and interpreting the Bible. It explores the remarkable journey of the Bible, from original text to modern translation, and will assist you to develop a more mature, complex understanding of the nature of its divine inspiration. It examines the many complex cultural and contextual issues that are essential in order to accurately apply the Bible's message.

This book is a must for ordinary Bible readers and serious students alike!

"*Making sense of the Bible*" is available in print or as an eBook from SmartFaith.net, Amazon and all major online retailers.

NO MORE MONKEY BUSINESS:
EVOLUTION IN CRISIS

"*No More Monkey Business*" is a concise, easy-to-read summary of the overwhelming and rapidly accumulating scientific evidence against evolution. Written with wit, and using simple layman's language, yet brimming with incontestable scientific evidence, this book highlights the huge problems now facing Darwin's original theory. Each chapter is full of fascinating scientific facts and discoveries which now directly contradict Darwin's naïvely simplistic theory proposed more than a century ago.

This book will challenge those who have unthinkingly assumed evolution to be a proven fact and will enable Christians to defend their faith with confidence.

"*No More Monkey Business*" is available in print or as an eBook from SmartFaith.net, Amazon and all major online retailers.

THE LITTLE BOOK OF CHURCH LEADERSHIP

The Little *book of*
CHURCH LEADERSHIP

A *little book with* BIG *ideas*

KEVIN SIMINGTON

"*The Little Book of Church Leadership*" is a little book with BIG ideas.

There is a crisis of leadership within the modern church. Not an *absence* of leadership. The modern church has plenty of leadership; just not the right sort. The kind of leadership that has evolved in many churches today is a long way from the leadership that was taught in the New Testament and practised by the first century church. This book is a call to seriously re-evaluate the church leadership style that has developed in recent years and return to the patterns and principles of church leadership as outlined in the New Testament.

"*The Little Book of Church Leadership*" is available in print or as an eBook from SmartFaith.net, Amazon and all major online retailers.

WELCOME TO THE UNIVERSE

How big is our solar system? Our galaxy? The universe? Does extraterrestrial life exist? How unique is Earth? Will we ever be able to travel to other stars? How realistic are the science fiction accounts of space travel?

"*Welcome To The Universe*" addresses these and many other issues of cosmic proportion. With stunning photographs and mind-boggling facts, "*Welcome To The Universe*" provides a fascinating glimpse into the wonders of the universe and the many challenges of space travel. It is the perfect 'pocket sized' compendium for budding astronomers and armchair lovers of science and science fiction.

"*Welcome To The Universe*" is available in print or as an eBook from SmartFaith.net, Amazon and all major online retailers.

SOMEONE ELSE'S LIFE

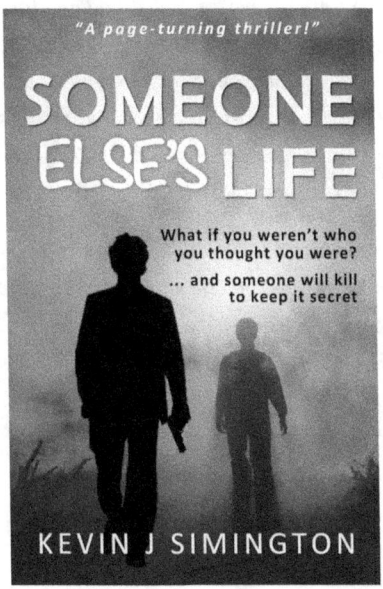

"A page-turning thriller by a master story-teller!"

Much more than a simple detective story, this is a complex portrayal of a good man who is pushed to extraordinary limits.

A mysterious case of identity switching turns deadly when struggling private investigator, John Targett, becomes involved. As John seeks to unravel one mystery, he is also forced to deal with an escalating menace when he becomes the target of a vicious gang whose path he has crossed. As the twin plots intertwine and the threats escalate, John is forced to take extreme measures to protect his daughter and fight for his own life. Plagued by his own demons and trying to raise his daughter alone, this is a beautifully crafted story of the lengths to which one man will go to protect those he loves. At times tender, filled with sparkling wit and peppered with edge-of-your-seat action, this is a multi-facetted mystery that will satisfy on many levels.

REVIEWS:

"An incredible thriller with the perfect twist! I adored this book. John Targett is my newest character crush! **Someone Else's Life** delivers on every front. It's delightful, witty, dangerous, and thought-provoking. The danger level is high throughout the novel, constantly raising the stakes and potentially making the reader breathless as events unfold. It's thrilling, and absolutely ends on the best possible note." Kat Cohen, Reviewer.

"Wow - this book is so much FUN! Great characters and a high-octane story that rips along until the twist you won't see coming on the last page. John Targett is an impressive new hero - tough and yet tender; highly skilled and often very funny. His laugh-out-loud interactions with his teenage daughter were one of my highlights." Darren Box, Amazon Review.

Available from: Amazon

THE STARPATH SERIES
KEVIN SIMINGTON

Consistently receiving 5-star reviews around the world!

A dying world. A desperate mission.

An unlikely hero.

"Incredibly well written, intelligent science fiction, by an author who really knows how to tell a story."

Book 1: THE STARS THAT BECKON

Book 2: THE STARS THAT BEND TIME

Book 3: A PATH THROUGH THE STARS

Book 4: Eden Rising

Available from Amazon

CONNECT WITH KEVIN SIMINGTON

Non-Fiction books and resources: SmartFaith.net

Fiction books: kevinsimington.com

Facebook: https://www.facebook.com/ReflectionsKev/

ABOUT THE AUTHOR

Kevin Simington is a theologian and apologist who is passionate about helping Christians grow deeper in their faith. He spent 31 years in Christian ministry, as a church pastor and a Christian educator. He is now a full time author and speaker. His website, SmartFaith.net, and Facebook page, "Reflections on Faith and Life", provide valuable resources for defending the Christian faith and equipping Christians. Kevin's weekly blog, available through his website and Facebook page, provides incisive commentary on social issues, theology, apologetics and ethics, and is read by thousands of people worldwide. He also writes for "My Christian Daily", an international Christian magazine.

NOTES

2. Understand The Wonder Of The Cross

1. Thallus – Third book of his history

3. Trust In Jesus As Saviour

1. https://www.law.cornell.edu/supremecourt/text/32/150

9. Trust The Bible's Reliability

1. Paul L. Maier, "Biblical Archaeology: Factual Evidence to Support the Historicity of the Bible", Christian Research Journal, volume 27, number 2 (2004)
2. BT, Sanhedrin 43a, quoted in https://en.wikipedia.org/wiki/Yeshu#Yeshu_the_sorcerer

www.ingramcontent.com/pod-product-compliance
Lightning Source LLC
Chambersburg PA
CBHW050308010526
44107CB00055B/2150